SUPPORTING FAMILIES

Children in Society Series
Edited by Stewart Asquith

Other titles:
Families and the Future

SUPPORTING FAMILIES

Edited by
Malcolm Hill, Rosalind Hawthorne Kirk and Diana Part

Series Editor: Stewart Asquith

HMSO: EDINBURGH

© Crown copyright
First published 1995

Applications for reproduction should be made to HMSO British Library
Cataloguing in Publication Data
A catalogue record for this book is available from the British Library

ISBN 0 11 495716 9

Contents

Acknowledgements	vii
Contributors	ix
Preface	xiii
1. The Impact of Changing Social Policies on Families 　*Rosalind Hawthorne Kirk and Diana Part*	1
2. Family Policies in Western Europe 　*Malcolm Hill*	17
3. Changing Families 　*Martin Richards*	39
4. Family Poverty and the Role of Family Support Work 　*Gil Long*	53
5. Families and the Law: Policing or Support? 　*Kathleen Marshall*	71
6. Family Support in Child Protection 　*Jane Gibbons*	87
7. Social Support and Early Years Centres 　*Rosalind Hawthorne Kirk*	99
8. Social Work Services for Young People 　*Malcolm Hill, John Triseliotis and Moira Borland*	119
9. Supporting Families Through Inter-Agency Work: 　Youth Strategies in Scotland 　*Andrew Kendrick*	135
10. Support to Families:- Dilemmas, Changes and Challenges 　*Malcolm Hill, Rosalind Hawthorne Kirk and Diana Part*	149
Index	159

ACKNOWLEDGEMENTS

WE would like to thank the contributors to this volume for their hard work and for keeping to tight deadlines in providing their chapters. The advice and encouragement of Alastair Holmes of HMSO and Stewart Asquith (Series Editor) have been much appreciated. The book was planned to mark the International Year of the Family in 1994 and at that time both Rosalind Hawthorne Kirk and Diana Part were working for Tayside Region Social Work Department. They would like to acknowledge the support given to them by the Department in this enterprise.

Malcolm Hill, Rosalind Hawthorne Kirk and Diana Part

CONTRIBUTORS

Moira Borland trained as a social worker and then worked for a number of years in Strathclyde Region, primarily with children and their families. She obtained an MSc in Advanced Social Work Studies at the University of Edinburgh. She now teaches on the Master in Social Work course at the University of Glasgow. Her research, reports and publications have centred on adoption, fostering, residential child care and social work services for teenagers.

Jane Gibbons is a Senior Research Fellow in the School of Health and Social Work at the University of East Anglia. She has worked previously as a probation officer, psychiatric social worker and social work teacher. Her main research interests have been in the social care of people with serious mental disorders and in family support and preventive services.

Rosalind Hawthorne Kirk is Head of Pre-Fives and Out of School Care (Social Work) in Central Regional Council. Prior to this, she worked for 11 years following graduation as a social worker in the Social Work Department of Tayside Regional Council where she was employed latterly as Principal Officer (Children and Young People). She has undertaken planning and evaluative work on child care and is currently conducting research on the relationships between social networks and social support and their impact on families using early years services. She has published papers on early years services and contributed to a book on the review of day care.

Malcolm Hill is a Senior Lecturer and Baring Fellow at the Centre for the Study of the Child & Society, University of Glasgow. He worked for Social Services Departments in London, before moving to Edinburgh to carry out research concerning parents and young children. For some years he has taught social work and social policy students and is currently organiser of a child care management course for Romanians. Recent research and publications have focused on adoption, young people in contact with social work services, comparative social policy and children with parents who have drink-related problems.

CONTRIBUTORS

Andrew Kendrick is Lecturer in Research Methods in the Department of Social Work, University of Dundee, and course co-ordinator for the postgraduate research student programme. He completed a PhD in Social Anthropology at the London School of Economics in 1984 and has carried out research leading to publications on a range of child care issues, including child in care reviews and residential child care. He is currently carrying out research on the implications of local government reorganisation for services to children and young people in difficulty.

Gil Long worked as a secondary teacher and in adult education with the Worker's Educational Association until 1987, when she became Training Adviser with Citizen's Advice Scotland. In 1992 she joined the Scottish Division of Save the Children Fund to set up the Child Poverty Resource Unit. The Unit seeks to publicise the extent and nature of child poverty in Scotland and works with SCF's community based projects to develop anti-poverty work.

Kathleen Marshall qualified as a solicitor in 1975 and worked initially in local government in Glasgow. In 1989 she was appointed Director of the Scottish Child Law Centre, a post she held for five years. She is currently Gulbenkian Fellow in Children's Rights at Glasgow University's Centre for the Study of the Child & Society, involved in research related to participation by children in decision-making. She is a council member of the Children's Rights Development Unit and of the Commission on Children and Violence. She is also Visiting Professor in Social Work to Glasgow Caledonian University.

Diana Part is Senior Lecturer and Course Director for the Diploma in Social Work programme at Northern College, Dundee. At the time the book was in preparation, she was Assistant Principal Officer for Foster Care and, before that for Child Protection, in Tayside Region. She has worked with children and their families as reviewing officer, through Child and Family Psychiatry, Adult Psychiatry and Child Care. She has carried out research on foster children.

Martin Richards is Director of the Centre for Family Research and Reader in Human Development at the University of Cambridge. His research has ranged widely over topics related to family life, but parental divorce and children has been a persistent theme. He is a Trustee of the Cambridge Family and Divorce Centre and has been active in developing comprehensive mediation techniques and counselling for children who have experienced parental separation. His books include *Infancy and the World of the Newborn* (1980); *Divorce Matters* (with J. Burgoyne and R. Ormrod, 1987); *Sexual Arrangements: Marriage and Affairs* (With J. Ribstein, 1992). The volume *The Troubled Helix: Social and Psychological Implications of the New Genetics* (co-edited with J. Marteau) is to be published by Cambridge University Press in 1995.

John Triseliotis is Professor Emeritus and Senior Research Fellow at the International Social Sciences Institute, University of Edinburgh. He was previously Professor of Social Work at the same university. Over the past 30 years he has undertaken many research studies and authored or co-authored books and articles, mainly in the areas of adoption, fostering and residential care. His most recent book, *The Theory and Practice of Foster Care*, is published by Batsford.

PREFACE

THE seeds of this book lie in Scotland and were planted in the International Year of the Family (1994), but the enterprise extends more widely. The original idea arose from connections amongst the editors who were then working for Tayside Regional Council (Rosalind Hawthorne Kirk and Diana Part) and the University of Glasgow (Malcolm Hill). We were enthusiastic about working collaboratively to mark the Year of the Family. Our common professional backgrounds as social workers meant that our particular interest in 'the family' centred on the role of agencies and services aimed at supporting families with dependent children. We were conscious of the many gaps and inadequacies in the support available to families, as well as the fact that some actions by professionals are experienced as unwelcome or intrusive. Therefore, it seemed valuable to review the needs of families and service responses in the light of the inherent tensions in the relationship between the state and the family, and in the context of many recent changes in the nature of welfare provision.

The chapters which follow include several which focus mainly on the situation in Scotland, although the implications are broader. Two chapters consider the UK as a whole, one is focused on England and one reports on a study which covered agencies in both England and Scotland. In addition, there is a chapter which provides a broader perspective by examining developments elsewhere in Western Europe. Besides this geographical mix, the book also includes the perspectives of contributors from different backgrounds, including social work, the law, anthropology, psychology and teaching. Some are currently engaged in service-delivery, others are academic researchers.

The main themes of the book are identified and discussed in Chapters 1 and 2, but it may be useful to outline briefly the key elements of each chapter first. After the overview of family policy issues in the first two chapters, attention turns to analyses of current family circumstances, with special emphasis on the poorest families in our society. The remaining chapters consider particular kinds of services and policies directed at families and children. These include reports on the findings of recent research.

In **Chapter 1**, Rosalind Hawthorne Kirk and Diana Part examine how changes in the British welfare state have impinged on families with children. They consider the implications of the commitment by Central Government to individualism, parental responsibility and minimum intervention. They note that vulnerable families have suffered most from the negative consequences like growth in poverty and reduced services, but been least able to benefit from positive consequences such as wider choice. These issues are examined in relation to each of the major welfare sectors, such as housing, health and education.

The next **Chapter** (2) introduces a comparative perspective by examining family policies in other countries of Western Europe. Malcolm Hill identifies the principal aims and mechanisms used by governments to support and influence families – usually, although not invariably, with benign intent. A classification of different models of family policy is presented and then variations in particular forms of financial benefits and services are considered. The chapter concludes with a glimpse of the growing trend towards internationalisation of family policy, as illustrated by the emergent role of the European Union in this respect.

Martin Richards reviews the changing nature of families and households in **Chapter 3**. He urges both concern and caution in viewing the current situation. Major changes have certainly taken place, but these are not so dire as some commentators would have us believe, nor necessarily negative in their consequences. Richards firstly outlines the evidence about developments in marriage, cohabitation, child-bearing and divorce, then considers their meaning and implications. He argues that social and economic policies should be based on careful understanding of general trends and attention to the needs of those who suffer as a result.

Chapter 4 makes clear that whatever their family relationships many children (and their parents) continue to suffer as a result of material want. Gil Long summarises the evidence that the number of children living in poverty has grown markedly in recent years. Causes include altered patterns of employment and restrictions in social security benefits. Poverty has major effects on children's daily life, health and education. Whilst many of these problems require a response at the societal level, Long ends with an example of how a neighbourhood project can improve families' economic situation and autonomy.

The first of the chapters which concentrate on public intervention (**Chapter 5**) teases out tensions in legal responses to family difficulties between social control and social support. Kathleen Marshall scrutinises the current Scottish child care law system. International influences are again apparent in the use as a standard of the UN Convention on the Rights of the Child, ratified by the UK in 1991. In relation to both private law (e.g. divorce) and public law (e.g. child protection), the state has to tread a thin line between excessive intrusion or 'policing' and ensuring that the interests and views of children are adequately taken into account. Marshall illustrates this dilemma with particular attention to the role of Safeguarders in the Scottish Children's Hearings System and of social workers in child abuse investigations.

Child protection is the focus of **Chapter 6**, this time within the context of legislation applying to England & Wales, namely the Children Act, 1989. Here Jane Gibbons notes that in principle this gave considerable scope for local authorities to meet the needs of families. However, resource constraints and the priority given to investigations of alleged child abuse have meant that services are often confined only to families identified as including children who have been harmed or are 'at risk'. Gibbons describes research which showed the widespread material and other needs of families in touch with Social Services, yet for the majority no positive services result at the end of the day. Instead major time resources are swallowed up by investigations and only the few identified as bearing serious risk warrant active help. This amply illustrates how the response to family poverty portrayed in Chapter 4 often consists of the 'social policing' rather than the 'social support' distinguished in Chapter 5.

The relationship between poverty and services is explored further in **Chapter 7**. Rosalind Hawthorne Kirk discusses what used to be known as pre-school day care and education, but is increasingly referred to as early years provision. After identifying the range of facilities and shortfall of places in relation to demand, she reports on the first stage of her own longitudinal study which examines the interplay between public services and social support. Contrasts are noted in the kinds of family using client-focused centres, neighbourhood centres and nursery schools. The services were highly valued by most families, many of whom had very low incomes and were subject to high stress levels. Rationing and organisational separation of services means that access is both restricted and divisive. Some families are thereby denied opportunities for social and economic integration.

The last two chapters move along the life course to consider families with teenage children. In **Chapter 8**, Malcolm Hill, John Triseliotis and Moira Borland suggest that their needs have taken a back seat because of the policy emphasis on ·child protection. They describe findings from their study of young people receiving social work services in five local authorities in England and Scotland. The sample included some supervised at home and others placed away from home in residential and foster care, as well as a number who experienced both. Most of the parents and young people were satisfied with the services provided, though there was often little choice. The availability of resources like group work, befriending and foster care vary greatly from area to area. The study identified a need for agency policies and inter-agency arrangements which target this age group more specifically and comprehensively.

Andrew Kendrick in **Chapter 9** explores how some local authorities in Scotland have attempted to do just that by producing youth strategies agreed jointly between social work and education departments, together with other agencies in some areas. He distinguishes a 'case-oriented' approach, focused on particular children with identified needs or difficulties, from 'community development' approaches intended to influence wider issues across whole areas or neighbourhoods. Implementation of the strategies has been uneven, but Kendrick describes some successful multi-disciplinary projects which have sought to work in partnership with families.

In the concluding chapter we draw out briefly some common themes and implications. We believe this volume demonstrates and illustrates how services can and do positively support families in their task of bringing up children, whilst pinpointing how improvements can be made.

Malcolm Hill, Rosalind Hawthorne Kirk and Diana Part

1

THE IMPACT OF CHANGING SOCIAL POLICIES ON FAMILIES

Rosalind Hawthorne Kirk and Diana Part

THE theme of this book, supporting families, draws together material from a range of contexts at a time when societies throughout the world are confronted by many global challenges – environmental, social, political and economic. Services to support families are firmly rooted in various beliefs about what constitutes a family and what should be its role and purpose. The family engenders different meanings and is itself characterised by diversity and change, as explored in some depth by Richards in Chapter 3. Throughout the book we are concerned primarily with support to nuclear families, comprising parent(s) and dependent children, although 'the family' in a wider sense also embraces relationships amongst adults in kin networks. Our aim is to identify and examine some of the influences which impact today on the family in the UK with prominence given in some chapters to the Scottish dimension. Reference is also made to influences from the European Union which have come increasingly to the fore. Our knowledge and understanding of each nation state has grown and has increased the opportunity for the exchange of ideas which lead to policy development. Although social policy changes have been resisted by the current government, increasing co-operation amongst nation states will make external pressures hard to ignore. Some of the issues which are high on the current family policy agenda across the European Union are discussed by Hill in the following chapter to set the scene for more detailed discussion of policies and practice in the UK. Consideration is also given to some of the responses made by the state to support families under stress, identifying issues to be addressed and making proposals for their future development. This introductory chapter aims to outline aspects of the wider picture surrounding the issues dealt with more fully throughout the book.

Pressures on the welfare state

The welfare state in the UK was set up following the Second World War in recognition of the experiences of widespread hardship, poverty and ill health, which were symptomatic of a wider economic malaise. At a time of national solidarity and unity, there was popular support for government to be proactive and interventionist to ensure that every citizen's basic needs were met. The nuclear family was seen as the most viable unit on which to base the framework for national investment in forthcoming generations as the potential workforce of the future. As a result sweeping changes were made to generate government income, including the creation of a national insurance scheme to enable health and other welfare services to be put in place.

The past fifteen to twenty years have seen fundamental and profound changes made to the welfare state. These have taken place within the context of world wide economic recession, demographic and social changes and shifts in public attitudes towards the role of state intervention in the lives of individuals and families. In the 1940s provision was established or consolidated, largely on a universal basis, to meet basic needs for health care, education, housing and subsistence income, supplemented by targeted support services, such as social work. In recent years, these have been confronted by escalating cost and growing demands. The welfare state was built upon a number of assumptions prevalent at the time. Ongoing economic growth and full employment were fundamental tenets which have been impossible to sustain, yet were essential to provide a manageable balance between investment in public services and demand for their use. Increased life expectancy, improved health of the majority of the population and technological advances have contributed to the pressures on the health and welfare services. Beliefs about the stability of the traditional nuclear family comprising male breadwinner, home-making wife and mother and their children with associated dependencies and unequal power distribution, have been severely challenged by the women's movement and shown to be no longer applicable today, if they ever were. The welfare state relied upon women's labour as unpaid carers, domestic workers and organisers of family life. This is no longer feasible nor acceptable as women's need to participate in the labour market has increased, although in practice many are in low paid, part-time work.

Views of children as 'belonging' to their parents and subjugated to their authority have also lost credence in the modern Western view of the world. Children are recognised as individuals in their own right with legitimate needs distinct from those of their parents. Public statements which reflect these principles have increased in frequency in recent years, although the application of this still has some way to go. In 1991 the UK government ratified a series of rights for children encompassing the provision of services, rights to protection and participation in decision making, when it adopted the UN Convention of Children's Rights (Newell, 1991; Asquith and Hill, 1994). The principles embodied within this international framework have served to challenge some of the assumptions held about the subordinate place of children in society and are now routinely referred to in policy documents on the family published by public bodies throughout the UK.

Mirroring these changes, there have been major shifts in perception of the role of parents from one in which rights and duties predominated towards one in which parental responsibilities towards their children are of prime importance. This was enshrined in law at the beginning of the 1990s in England and Wales (Children Act, 1989) and also features prominently in the Children (Scotland) Bill which is currently under consideration with proposed enactment in 1996.

These changes in public perception of the rights of each family member are compatible with the growth in individualism as well as the recognition of the intrinsic worth of all individuals and their rights as citizens. Public and political support converges on the broader rhetoric of the importance of the individual within society but there are inherent tensions for the family as a unit when the interests of individual members conflict. This is apparent as an issue in cases of child protection where the intervention of the state can be interpreted both as one which is essential to the best interests of the vulnerable child and also as an inappropriate intrusion into the privacy of the family and undermining of the rights of parents. The ambivalence of these attitudes towards the protection of children is often played out through the media, criticising authorities for lack of intervention in some instances and over zealous approaches in others. The conflicts between the rights of individual family members can also become evident at times of divorce and separation, especially when resolution is sought within the framework of the law which is inherently adversarial.

Similarly, tensions arise when the wider distribution of power is threatened through the empowerment of individuals belonging to disadvantaged groups such as women, the disabled, ethnic minorities or gay activists. The ability to exercise individual rights which challenge the status quo may only proceed at a pace determined, within fairly tightly constrained limits, by various combinations of legislation and policy supported by powerful vested interests and public opinion. Recognition of disadvantage amongst such groups can be seen by some as threatening to society as a whole because it legitimises challenges to the distribution of power within other social institutions, such as the family which is so often seen as a foundation for social integration. Throughout all the discussion of changing social policies and their effects on families there is one constant. For almost every example of change or reduction of services for families the difficulties for black families are greater than those described for the rest of the population (Brown, 1984; Bahl 1994). It is beyond the scope of this book to look at the black perspective in particular but it must be borne in mind when reading every chapter that the supports available for families of minority ethnic origins are less accessible and often poorly planned and implemented with respect to their particular needs. The views of the black community have seldom been studied taking the needs of the users, their culture, race, and communication needs in mind. (Dominelli, 1988; Ridley and Kendrick, 1994).

The impact of Thatcherism

The welfare state as it was first set up, laudable though it was at the time, had to be transformed if it was to remain viable and pertinent to the current climate and this process had already begun before the Thatcher government began its radical programme of change from the early 1970s. The force behind the thinking of the right was to promote individualism and self reliance and thereby reduce dependence on the state. A position of minimalist intervention was adopted in both economic and social welfare policies, drawing increasingly heavily on dominant policy perspectives in the United States. The approach taken by Thatcher and Major governments has been to assume increased centralised control over welfare and local government, adopting new methods of organising services in an attempt to reduce public expenditure, amounting to around fifty percent of the nation's wealth (Midwinter,1994). Fixed annual budgets, privatisation, contracting out services and the development of internal markets have all become commonplace ways of applying the philosophy of market forces to the public sector in an attempt to balance the match between needs, demands and resources. This type of management, when applied to the provision of personal health and welfare services, has significant implications for the family. Some of these are discussed below while the extent of others are yet to be fully realised and understood.

Midwinter (1994) argues that centralisation has been the most prominent feature of Thatcherite policies. Central government has exerted increasingly strict control over local government services through rate capping and increased reliance on central funding for local services. Public expenditure has been reduced, thus diminishing services for families which local authorities provide.

The idea of minimal state intervention extends to families, whose concerns are viewed as essentially private unless the behaviour of members is deemed as destructive or disruptive to the wider society or parenting is so inadequate as to be potentially damaging to their children. When health problems are seen as the root cause or behaviour is illegal, an individualised response by the police, Courts or health services commonly results. The family as a unit can also become the focus of intervention by public authorities such as housing and social services because of the beliefs about the roles of parents, mothers in particular, which were encompassed in the policies of the welfare state. Families with greater access to resources are more able to maintain privacy than those who are poor and dependent on the state for income maintenance, housing and so on. This is not only because they can afford to buy alternative ways to overcome or mask difficulties, it is also because the poor are obliged to open up their lives and reveal personal information to prove eligibility to gain access to many essential services.

The economy and income maintenance

Although economic productivity has increased, economic growth is no better than it was at the earlier stages of the new right take-over, due to the decline in manufacturing and the rise in unemployment over this period (around an official figure of three million, although it has been unofficially estimated at double this), contributing to a social security bill in 1991/92 of over £58 billion (Midwinter,1994). At the same time as poverty and disadvantage increased for a sizeable minority of the population, the living standards of the other third had risen accounting for some of the ambivalence experienced today towards increased taxation to support growing public expenditure. Between 1979 and 1991, the income of the average household rose by thirty six percent while the income of those in the bottom ten percent fell by fourteen percent. In Chapter 4, Long explores the growing poverty amongst families with dependent children which has increased rapidly alongside long term unemployment and a low wage economy resulting in rapid increases in the working poor who are employed in low paid, often part time work. The weekly household incomes of growing numbers of families are insufficient to meet their child care and subsistence needs and as a result they have become entrapped in a spiral of dependence on the state. She highlights how doubly disadvantaged some families are, such as those belonging to ethnic minorities, those headed by lone mothers or with disabled members, showing how many of these families are disproportionately represented amongst the poorest members of society. A further assault on some families, particularly those headed by a lone parent, has been the introduction of the Child Support Agency. The rationale of this controversial legislation is to ensure that absent parents (usually fathers) fulfil their financial responsibilities towards their families.

Other recent changes to the systems of income maintenance, based on an assumption of delayed adulthood, have contributed both to the growing poverty amongst families and to youth homelessness. For example, the financial dependence on parents of young people from the age of 16 years to 18 years was extended when their eligibility to Income Support was removed. Families have to manage on less within an increasingly individualistic and materialistic society with resultant stresses which require intervention at the national, community and individual levels if family support is to be effective. However, those who are in positions of power to effect such changes have been faring better in the current climate, resulting in a diminished political and public will to continue to fund growing demand for welfare services through traditional methods of taxation. This has been evident in the manifestos of all political parties whose policies are increasingly convergent, with solutions which involve rationing and a mixed economy of care being supported or at least unopposed by all political persuasions. The 'affordable welfare state' remains one of the primary challenges for the government of the day (George and Miller, 1994).

Housing

The dramatic changes towards increased owner occupation were made possible by changes to housing legislation in the 1980s which enabled local authority tenants to buy their homes at favourable rates and to opt for a landlord other than the local authority if they lived in a council estate. By 1988 around a fifth of council properties had been transferred to private ownership. The public housing stock which remained was in poor condition and the standards required to replace and upgrade were substantial. The incentives, as well as the financial capacity, to continue to build public housing which could then potentially create profits for the private sector has led to a transformation in the housing market, reducing the availability of public housing and compounding homelessness which has increased markedly. Local authorities no longer have the capacity to respond to the needs of families who would have chosen to live in local authority accommodation, as their parents may have done, nor are they able to fulfil much of their statutory obligations to meet the housing needs of families in crisis such as those experiencing domestic violence. Housing difficulties are increasingly viewed as a result of individual inadequacy or vulnerability, with responsibility becoming increasingly directed towards the voluntary sector and social services.

Transport

Changing patterns of travel and transport have also impacted on families. Public transport has been deregulated and transport policies have been mainly focused on car travel. Beuret (1991) argues that transport policies discriminate against families particularly those on low incomes. Families without a car have become increasingly disadvantaged as the trend to out of town shopping in superstores or hypermarkets away from town centres creates difficulties for shoppers without their own transport. This is especially so for mothers with young children who are more likely to shop locally on foot. The reduction of local and corner shops has made shopping more difficult and more expensive. The small shops cannot take advantage of the economies of scale which the multiples and large stores use to their advantage.

The number of families with a car is growing. In 1961 three in ten households in the UK had a car, whereas in 1991 only three in ten were without one (Social Trends 1994). For those families with a car there is less use of it by the women and other members of the family than by the men who typically use it to travel to work (Beurat, 1991). For families headed by one parent only, car ownership is much lower than for those families with two adults. In 1986 less than a quarter (24.2%) of families of one adult and one child owned a car. The figure for a family of two adults and two children was 84% (Family Expenditure Survey, 1986). The deregulation of public transport has also led to reductions in some routes, particularly those in rural areas which are not as cost effective (Amos 1994). This further disadvantages low income rural families.

Health Services

Significant changes have occurred in the organisation and provision of health services in the UK in the past decade which have radically altered the delivery of health care. These include the development of non-medical health service managers, the splitting of services into purchasers or providers and the forming of NHS trusts. The Patient's Charter set standards for waiting lists and other services and has produced more information about different health authorities. In some instances these changes may have led to improvement in services to families but not all are for the better. The erosion of free access is leading to a greater divide between those who can readily use health services and those who cannot. Charges for eye testing, increased dental charges and prescriptions have further eroded the original aim of a free National Health Service. The market system introduced by the NHS and Community Care Act, (1990) established a split between purchasers and providers of health care. The result is a pluralistic system with competition a central tenet. Kurtz and Tomlinson (1994) argue that this reorganisation of the National Health Service as an internal market is creating serious difficulties, particularly for integrated services, for multi-disciplinary work and for the exercise of true parental choice.

An early change began with the reduction of local hospitals which offered beds for obstetrics and paediatrics. Women, especially those in rural areas, had much further to travel to give birth or to be with their sick children, often in hospitals not of their choosing. This, coupled with the recent reduction of time spent in hospital puts even greater pressure on families. They have further to travel before, during and after hospitalisation and for appointments. Following discharge more care is needed for the patient at home than before. If the patient is a woman there is frequently an assumption that she will pick up the homemaking tasks with no convalescent time.

In addition, there have been reductions in home visiting by general practitioners to sick family members which has further diminished support to families. General practitioners now have restrictions placed on the drugs they can prescribe. With the fund holding practices in particular there are fears that in the future treatments may or may not be offered depending on the cost of that treatment rather than the medical need.

The greatest impact however has followed the implementation of the NHS and Community Care Act 1990. That changed the emphasis of the 1970s and 1980s of moving towards care in the community to being cared for by the community. The closure of long stay hospitals for the frail elderly, infirm, chronically sick and people with a psychiatric illness or disability has sent many out of these institutions to be cared for by their families, if they have them. Once there, despite the efforts of local authorities, the support and resources offered are frequently minimal. This leaves a great burden of care on those families, the women especially, to care for their dependant relatives. As this frequently means giving up employment, the loss of income can disadvantage the whole family.

The care of dependants emphasised as a family commitment saves money for the Treasury, but diminishes the value of care. The independence required of society by government ministers attacking the 'dependency culture' has led to families caring for members who need far more than tender loving care. The recent move to institute payment for those in long stay nursing homes – those who would formerly have remained in hospital – will put great stress on the other family members.

The emphasis on value for money and the need for health trusts to manage tight budgets has been accompanied by a move towards targeting rather than universality of services. There is a threat to the availability of health visiting services to all families with children under school age. The health visitor seeing the family in their home is a valued part of the support network offering support, advice, monitoring and has the opportunity for preventative work (Blackburn,1994). A similar loss is involved in the proposals in some areas to limit school medical services to those children deemed to be at risk.

There are, however, also positive changes in health services that are giving families more support. Children with disabilities have long been on the periphery of health and care services but recent partnerships between agencies, parents and the children have given them greater consideration in service provision. The Audit Commission (1994) argued for universal provision of family support services to reduce stress on families and diminish the need for crisis intervention. Respite care for children and their parents or carers is now a higher priority although there is still far to go to achieve the range of provision required. The requirement to produce joint child care plans involving social service or social work departments, education and health services is a positive step which could compensate for some of the fragmentation of services.

Health promotion strategies have been developed as alternative methods of approaching the escalating costs of the treatment of ill-health. Originally targeted mainly at ante-natal care there is more emphasis now on post-natal care and beyond. Breast feeding clinics, anti-smoking campaigns and services for young people or families with addiction problems can all serve to encourage or support the family constellation. Information needs to take more account of the circumstances of families on low incomes. For instance, some of the advice given on nutrition and healthy eating is for foodstuffs they cannot afford.

Education

Education policies have also undergone major changes over the past decade. The two main themes apparent from these policies are parental choice and devolved management of schools. Self government for schools has also been important in English education but has failed to establish any momentum in Scotland.

The way schools are managed has been radically changed by a series of measures – placing requests for schools outwith the catchment area, the Parents' Charter, the publication and dissemination of examination results, legislation on School Boards, opting out and proposed legislation over unauthorised absences. Many of these measures have enhanced parents' rights and given parents more knowledge about and possibility of involvement with schools. Now that schools have been given responsibility for their functions and their own success there is a danger, however, that pastoral care and support for the more vulnerable pupils may be in jeopardy. With schools ever more conscious of public scrutiny of their achievements and examination results, those children who need individual attention and more from the school than education may be unable to get the time, attention and care they require. They may be further disadvantaged by the very changes to the educational system which were heralded as supports to families.

The Parent's Charter, as David (1993) points out, is based on middle class educational standards and does not address issues of race, gender or class. She argues that the reforms, although defining the parent as the key customer or consumer of education, will only help a minority of families. Only those families with prior knowledge and resources will be able to take up the possibility of empowerment with the chances of improved educational progress for their children that might follow.

The consumerist model now in place is based on the assumption that all consumers can exercise the same influence. The system of placing requests for schools becomes irrelevant for families living on low incomes in both rural and urban areas with poor public transport and no transport of their own. The system of publishing examination results may also disadvantage such families. The present arrangement of making public only crude results regardless of the children's starting positions will strengthen those schools with an intake of academically oriented pupils. Those families who have the resources will make placing requests to the schools with good results. The local schools will lose some of the stronger pupils and their subsequent results will look less positive. The divide between the 'good' schools and the others will increase, leaving the latter with fewer resources and lower morale. There is however a move to have an 'added value' dimension added to the publication of exam results. This will help to identify those schools who work hard on behalf of their pupils of all standards and make progress with children who are disadvantaged and yet may not achieve high academic results. It may do a little towards keeping the wider definition of education as 'preparation for the work of life'. (OED, 1970). The National Curriculum obliges schools in England to 'prepare pupils for the opportunities, responsibilities and experiences of adult life' (Department of Education and Science. 1988). However there is little evidence of a co-ordinated approach to family life education (Rowe and Whitty, 1993) and there is an argument that to achieve a reduction of school age pregnancies a school based health education is required as part of preparation for parenthood (N.F.E.R., 1993).

Changing policy has brought a new emphasis on partnership with parents. Few schools have had a strong tradition of welcoming and involving parents. It has yet to be seen, however, if these changes bring fewer benefits than costs to children whose families are living on the margin. School Boards have not had the impact anticipated, although arguably they have increased parents' rights. The record of supporting children's rights in the educational system is poor. It may well be that the children who start their lives disadvantaged find that they are compounded further in the educational system which is now moving away from the comprehensive philosophy and rewarding those with advantage (Taylor-Gooby, 1994).

One move in the opposite direction from partnership appears to be the increasing number of children who are being excluded from schools, particularly primary schools. This can only serve to increase stress for the families of these children as well as significantly disadvantaging the children. In a study by Parsons (1994), it was found that excluded children lost more than three-quarters of a year's schooling on average. The typical excluded child had to wait 14 weeks for home tuition and then it was for only three hours per week.

One change for the better has been the increasing attention paid to children with special needs and those with disabilities. In this field a genuine partnership with parents has begun alongside collaboration with other agencies. Also a number of areas have developed youth strategies in which multi-agency groups are working with parents and young people to improve educational opportunities at individual and community levels (see Kendrick, Chapter 9).

Early years provision

Supporting families through the provision of services to young children has been treated as a marginal activity for many years by successive governments, reflecting an ambivalence towards state intervention in an area considered to be an essentially private, parental responsibility (Williams, 1989). Although there has been considerable central government investment in research and guidance on the protection of young as well as older children, the same is not true of either preventive or therapeutic services as Gibbons describes in Chapter 6. It has been left to local authorities to decide how much, and in what way, they should invest in early years services within a mixed economy of care and education. Commercial interests are currently shaping the development of new services as the numbers of women who are recruited into the labour market increases. Provision remains diverse and fragmented. Although the Children Act 1989 extended and strengthened the regulatory responsibilities of local authorities, the continued absence of a coherent, national strategy leaves wide variation in access and quality. Over the last decade much attention has been given to the need to improve co-ordination, but this has been hampered by the lack of joint mechanisms in central government (Pugh, 1988). Some of the factors, such as poverty, which impact on the type of local authority service received by some families with young children are more fully explored later by Hawthorne-Kirk in Chapter 7 who contrasts use and support of different kinds of services.

Crime and social control

Midwinter, 1994, reported that crime in England and Wales had increased by 36% over 10 years to 15 million incidents. The responses to this growing crime rate were of a similar centralist nature to those found in other public sector services. The number of police forces has decreased and the representation of elected councillors on police boards has been reduced. The introduction of privatisation into some aspects of police security work and the prison service have been accompanied by a growth in voluntarism through schemes such as Neighbourhood Watch, strengthening the mixed economy within policing.

The approaches to young people in trouble are different north and south of the border. In Scotland following implementation of the Social Work (Scotland) Act, 1968, a 'welfare' approach was adopted towards young offenders in common with those who are viewed as vulnerable and in need of protection. Children and young people about whom there are grounds for concern may be referred to the Reporter to the Children's Panel, which comprises lay members of the public trained to administer formal proceedings in the place of a juvenile court. Although the Hearings system has an interface with the Sheriff Court and criminal justice system, it is an essentially family based approach. It was placed under attack following Lord Clyde's (1992) inquiry into the removal of children from their parents in Orkney for providing insufficient recognition to the rights of both children and parents. However, it retains substantial support and there are recommendations in the Children (Scotland) Bill to improve and strengthen the system. Indeed its role is to be extended by bringing young offenders up to the age of 18 years within its remit to delay involvement with adult systems. In England and Wales solutions to the growing crime rate have been sought in strengthening punitive approaches to young people who offend, providing accommodation or family support for those within the welfare system and youth training for those within the criminal juvenile justice system. The discussion by Marshall in Chapter 5 is based on this Scottish system. She points out some of the ambiguities in this framework and in the processes which give rise to the enforcement and practice of social control of the family.

Social work and social services

Social services have never been prominent on the political agenda of any party. Recent public and media debates on both child protection and community care might indicate otherwise, but the response has largely been of rhetoric and regulation with little commitment to adequate resourcing to meet growing demands and needs (George and Miller, 1994). Gibbons in Chapter 6 provides evidence of the imbalance of the approaches taken by local authority social services to families, with an emphasis and concentration of resources on the investigation of children suspected of being maltreated or neglected at the expense of providing supportive services of a broader based nature. Hill, Triseliotis and Borland observe in Chapter 8 that services for adolescents have likewise taken a back seat as attention has focused almost exclusively on child protection. Like Kendrick (Chapter 9), they emphasise how intervention can be effective when social care and social work are combined with appropriate education.

The NHS and Community Care Act, 1990, brought with it new duties and responsibilities towards an increasingly ageing and vulnerable population, with a corresponding shift in priorities and resources away from the provision of services to families in the absence of sufficient funding to meet all the growing demands of an increasingly stressed society.

> *Central government makes the essential decisions determining how much will be available for the personal social services. But it makes them with only a broad and technical reference to social need. It also decides the duties and objectives of the services. Local authorities must do the best they can to fulfil their legal obligations within the funds made available to them. They can usually only spend more on one service by cutting another.* (Baldock, 1994, p.162.)

Baldock goes on to argue that needs as determined by demography and individual circumstances are only one of many factors which shape provision. Others include professional and public opinion, local government organisation and finance and local politics. Unlike other public services, social work was never envisaged as a universal service and wide variations in the levels of services across local authority and national boundaries are evidence of the range of pressures influencing provision rather than differences in patterns of need. The family, women in particular, have been relied upon to undertake vast amounts of caring work but their capacity to continue to do so is now under threat yet the implications of this have not been fully appreciated in resourcing and planning social service developments. Ring fencing of funds for community care and training have both contributed to ensuring that local social work and services departments obtain the amount of money decided by central government, both strengthening their position in relation to other local government departments at the same time as conforming to central government control.

Services to offenders and their families in Scotland have recently been extracted from the control of local authorities and been subject to centralised control and funding in a way that other social work services have not yet been. Fragmentation has been increased across the range of social work services – across client groups and within them – by separating the assessment and provision of services. Increasingly the role of many local authorities is to 'enable' and regulate provision in the voluntary and independent sectors.

Other current aspects of social work and social service support to families under stress are explored within the rest of this book. The long term impact of the changes we are currently undergoing will require to be viewed historically to be fully appreciated. In the meantime the capacity of individuals and families to respond to the speed, diversity and unpredictability of change is tested to the full, forcing adaptation in order to survive.

References

Amos, V. (1994) The EOC: Taking account of rural women in Scotland. In conference report *Equal opportunities for rural women in Scotland.* Glasgow: EOC.

Asquith, S. and Hill, M. (eds.) (1994) *Justice for Children*, Dordrecht: Martinus Nijhof.
Audit Commission. (1994) *Seen but not heard. Co-ordinating community child health and social services for children in need.* London: HMSO.
Bahl, K.(1994) The EOC: Taking account of black and ethnic minority women. In conference report *Equal opportunities for black and ethnic minority women in Scotland.* Glasgow: EOC.
Baldock, J. (1994) The personal social services: The politics of care. In V. George and S. Miller(eds.) *Social Policy Towards 2000: Squaring the Welfare Circle.* London and New York : Routledge.
Beuret, K. (1991) Women and transport. In Maclean, M. and Groves, D. (eds.) *Women's Issues in Social Policy.* London: Routledge.
Blackburn, C. (1994) In sickness and in health. In T. David (ed.) *Working Together for Young Children.* London: Routledge.
Brown, C. (1984) *Black and White Britain.* London: Heinemann.
Central Statistical Office (1994). *Social Trends 24.* London: HMSO.
Clyde Report (1992) *The Report of the Inquiry into the Removal of Children from Orkney in February 1991.* Edinburgh: HMSO.
David, M. (1993) The citizen's voice in education: parents, gender and education reform. In R. Page and J. Baldock (eds.) *Social Policy Review 5*, Social Policy Association, London.
Department of Education and Science. (1988). *The Education Reform Act 1988.* London: HMSO.
Department of Health and Social Security (1991) *Growing Older.* London: HMSO.
Dominelli, L. (1988) *Anti-racist Social Work,* London: Macmillan.
Family Expenditure Survey (1986) London HMSO – Quoted in Beuret, K. (1991) Women and transport. In Maclean, M. and Groves, D. (eds.). *Women's Issues in Social Policy,* London: Routledge.
George, V. and Miller, S. (1994) *Social Policy Towards 2000: Squaring the Welfare Circle.* London and New York : Routledge.
Hambleton, R. and Taylor, M. Transatlantic urban policy transfer. *Policy Studies* 15(2) 4–18.
Harrison, W. D. and Johnson, M. S. Child welfare policy in the United States. *Social Policy and Administration* 28(2) 139–150.
Kurtz, Z. and Tomlinson, J. (1991) How do we value our children today? As reflected by children's health, health care and policy? *Children and Society* 5:3, pp. 207–224.
Little, V. and Tomlinson, J. (1993) Education: thirty years of change – for better or for worse? In *Thirty Years of Change for Children.* (ed.). Pugh, G. London: National Children's Bureau.
Midwinter, E. (1994) *The Development of Social Welfare.* Buckingham and Philadelphia : Open University Press
National Foundation for Educational Research (1993) *A Survey of Health Education Policies in Schools.* London: Health Education Authority.
Newell, P. (1991) *The UN Convention and Children's Rights in the UK.* London: National Children's Bureau.
Parsons, C. (1994) *Excluding Primary School Children.* London: Family Policy Studies Centre.
Pugh, G. (1988) *Services for Under Fives.* London: National Children's Bureau.
Ridley, J. and Kendrick, A. (eds.) (1994) *Is Scotland colour blind? Race and research in Scotland.* Dundee: SSRG–Scotland.

Rowe, G. and Whitty, G. (1993) Five themes remain in the shadows. *Times Educational Supplement* 9.4. 8.

Shorter Oxford English Dictionary. (1970) Third edition.

Taylor-Gooby, P. (1994) Education – national success and individual opportunity. In George, V. and Miller, S. (eds.) *Social Policy Towards 2000: Squaring the Welfare Circle*. London: Routledge.

Williams, F. (1989) *Social Policy: A Critical Introduction*. Cambridge & Oxford: Polity Press and Basil Blackwell.

2

FAMILY POLICIES IN WESTERN EUROPE[1]

Malcolm Hill

Introduction

OVER the last 100 years, all the countries of Western Europe have developed policies and services aimed at supporting families, but these vary greatly in their nature and rationales. Comparisons between the UK and its closest neighbours help us to see whether there are lessons we can learn, both in overall approach and in detailed policy mechanisms.

Mechanisms of family policy

There are a number of difficulties in identifying and comparing overall patterns of family support. In the first place, measures directed at families are not always clearly labelled that way. Certain countries are said to have explicit family policies, because of statements in their constitutions (e.g. Germany, Ireland) or the existence of a single government ministry dealing with family affairs (e.g. Luxembourg). By contrast, countries like the UK are regarded as having largely implicit family policies, since basic principles are not codified and ministerial responsibility is dispersed. In most countries there is a mix of programmes both for families as a whole and also targeted towards particular family members, notably children or women. There are also many policies which have a major impact on families even though their primary purpose concerns something else, such as employment, transport or the environment. One of the most significant ways in which the state has taken over family functions is in the sphere of formal education, but this is usually treated separately from other services for families with children.

There are four main mechanisms by which the state intervenes in family life:
- *Regulation* – legislation, policy proposals, government statements e.g. on divorce, child welfare, abortion

---

[1] Western Europe is taken to comprise the twelve member states of the European Union in 1994 (including Greece which is geographically situated in south-east Europe) plus the new 1995 entrants (Sweden, Finland and Austria), together with Switzerland and Norway whose citizens voted to remain outside the Union.

- *Services* e.g. pre-school care, family centres, health clinics, foster and residential care
- *Financial payments* e.g. child benefit, income support, housing or educational allowances, assistance for child care costs
- *Indirect financial asssistance* e.g. payments to employers to assist with compensation during parental leave, child care tax relief

From time to time countries make significant shifts from one mechanism to another. For instance in 1989 the Netherlands government decided to abolish child tax allowances and instead devote the cash to expanding day care services (Moss, 1990). International comparisons also reveal that governments make policy decisions *not to take action*, revealed for example in the absence of rights in the UK to paid parental leave which is available in all the Scandinavian countries.

Aims of family policies

The measures taken ostensibly to assist families have varied in aims and justifications both from place to place and from one time to another. The most important have been to:

- influence the birth rate
- reduce disparities in incomes between households with and without children
- relieve family poverty
- sustain family unity or responsibility
- invest in the future generation
- meet labour market needs
- support gender equality and the management of work-family responsibilities
- safeguard the welfare of children when family disruption threatens or occurs

Not uncommonly, the same measure may be used to fulfil a number of different objectives. The history of family allowances and child benefit in the UK shows that at different times this form of payment has been supported for each one of the reasons listed above (see e.g. MacNicol, 1978; Deakin, 1988).

The principle of '*natalism*', i.e. boosting the birth rate has frequently been invoked as a reason for financial assistance to compensate for the costs of childbirth and childrearing. In fact all the evidence is that the impact on fertility is at best marginal. There has been a strong concern about birth rates in France, as a result of relative low population growth and military defeats in the 19th and early 20th centuries. This accounts in part for the long tradition of generous French family allowances which have therefore had a wider constituency of support than in Britain (Baker, 1986). Measures to sustain the population were included in French family policy objectives enunciated in the national plans of the 1970s and 1980s (Girod et al., 1985). Greece introduced additional payments for families with 3 or more children in 1990 because of concerns about its low birth rate.

The concept of the *'equalisation of burdens'* between the childless and those with children has been most explicitly used in Germany and Austria, though the principle underpins family policy elsewhere too. Austrian family allowances, free school travel and free school books were introduced in the 1950s out of a desire to transfer money to those with the 'burden' of maintaining children from adults who do not have children yet 'consciously or unconsciously derive benefit from the fact that others do so for them' (Munz and Wintersberger, 1987 p. 223). Benefits were also introduced to compensate mothers for loss of earnings while raising children. In Germany social insurance payments are made at levels related to previous earnings when mothers are absent from work to give birth to children and look after them. Such allowances are made in recognition of the extra costs of keeping children, income foregone and costs imposed by society (e.g. compulsory education). Germany also has very generous tax relief for individuals with children, although the precise entitlements vary because they are determined at the level of the individual states (Lander) of the Federal Republic (Dumon, 1992; Hantrais, 1994a).

Relief of family poverty is a stated objective of most social security systems. This represents vertical distribution of income (from the better off to poor families), as opposed to horizontal distribution from the childless to families with children. According to Dumon (1992), in recent years there has been a general trend away from supporting all families towards targeting those defined as being most in need.

Tackling family poverty was the principal rationale for Family Income Supplement, introduced in the UK during the early 1970s and later modified to become Family Credit. This is means-tested and graduated. An alternative approach is to have a guaranteed minimum income. In France the R.M.I. (Revenu minimum d'insertion) was introduced in 1988, so that poor families are given a payment which brings their income up to a minimum level (Grignon, 1993). Several members of the European Union have means-tested housing allowances in recognition of the significance of housing costs for low income families. In Germany, these vary according to family size (Ford and Chakrabarti, 1987). The absence of assistance towards housing costs in countries like Greece and Portugal greatly reduces the impact of their financial support for families with children (Bradshaw et al., 1993).

Ideas about family preservation have influenced government attitudes to public day care in a number countries. For instance UK provision has largely been limited to needy or 'at risk' target groups to relieve stress and hopefully prevent breakdown, whilst universal provision on demand has been resisted lest it undermine parental responsibilities (Land and Parker, 1978). This is also a factor which has distinguished Norway from the rest of Scandinavia. The much more limited Norwegian state involvement in child care compared with its neighbours has been justified by appeals to norms of family responsibility (Leira, 1993). Most countries have preferred to give financial support to make it easier for lone parents to stay home as this was seen as preferable for care of the children, compared with providing day care to facilitate paid employment. This policy has often engendered long term poverty for such households because the level of benefits has usually been well below full-time earnings (Duskin, 1990). Norwegian lone parents are eligible for high benefits and tax allowances so they have genuine choice about whether to stay home or work without there being a major income difference. This policy has meant that few lone parents households are in poverty, though there is also a low and declining rate of labour force participation (Kamerman and Kahn, 1987). In contrast a special Dutch allowance for lone parents is intended to encourage them to work.

Similarly government fiscal policies have often been based on presumptions of male breadwinner roles and have aggregated family resources (Dominelli, 1991). Tax allowances exist in several countries for spouses who stay at home and this tends to reinforce traditional role divisions. Luxembourg has a benefit for mothers who interrupt their careers to educate their children (Dumon, 1992). Separate taxation of men and women was introduced in Sweden in 1970 but not in Belgium, Spain or the UK until nearly 20 years later.

Services which are intended to benefit children (including schools) are commonly regarded as a worthwhile *investment for the future*. In the Benelux countries and France widespread provision is available to provide early stimulation and socialisation for children from the age of three onwards. Many Danish experts and parents believe that day care also confers early educational benefits on younger children, provided it is well resourced and professionally run. Hence in Denmark there has been a major investment in high quality day care and 40% of children under 3 attend publicly funded services (Moss, 1988; Vedel-Petersen, 1991). A somewhat more coercive approach to improving child health and welfare has been the French policy of making entitlement to cash benefits conditional on attendance at ante-natal services.

The *promotion of gender equality* was a feature in Eleanor Rathbone's campaign for family allowances in Britain during the 1930s, but has only become a major plank in broader family policy in the last 30 years.

Commitment to gender equality is most evident in Scandinavia (Kamerman and Kahn, 1992; Olsson and McMurphy, 1993). The main mechanisms adopted in the countries of Western Europe have consisted of equal opportunities employment legislation, provision of day care and after-school services, and indirect financial assistance (parental leave and tax concessions). Finland has granted a legal right to state funded day care in a family or centre setting for all children under school age in order to facilitate both early learning and parental employment (Leira, 1993).

Since gender inequalities in career paths become especially apparent after childbirth, several countries have introduced parental leave entitlements. Whereas in the UK, Ireland and southern Europe maternity leave entitles only women to absence from work with partial financial compensation, parental leave may be taken by either parent or by both in combination or sequence. In Sweden parental leave may be taken for up to 360 days in the first 4 years after childbirth, with an allowance worth 90% of previous earnings. Interestingly, Sweden was one of the few Western countries to have had an increase in fertility in the 1980s, although there was no explicit pro-natalist policy. This may be because measures introduced for other reasons (gender equality, access to work) have made it easier than elsewhere for women to combine motherhood with employment.

Meeting labour market needs has been a prominent factor influencing willingness to pay for measures with more avowedly family-oriented aims. Thus it has been argued that state financial payments to families reduce the need for employers to pay a family wage, hence reducing their labour costs. This contributed to the introduction of family allowances both in France and the UK (Jones, 1985). Governments have generally been more willing to expand early years services or give tax concessions for child care costs during periods of specific or general labour shortages (Tizard et al., 1976). In Sweden and Denmark a symbiosis has developed between public services and women's employment opportunities, since most women work in the public sector which in turn provides their child care (Siim, 1990).

For centuries the Church and more recently the state recognised the need to assume *quasi-parental responsibility* for orphans and for children who for other reasons cannot stay with their parents (Gottesmann, 1990). Most of Northern and Western Europe have seen a major shift from residential care to substitute family placements, but even for young children the main option remains institutional care in many parts of southern Europe (Colton and Hellinckx, 1994; Triseliotis, 1994).

Child protection systems everywhere face dilemmas between family privacy and surveillance, between children's rights to protection and parent's rights to non-interference. By and large elsewhere in Europe there is more reliance on voluntary cooperation with families than the ready resort to the law which has characterised policy and practice in Britain. In part, this is because child protection has escaped the intense public and media scrutiny which has been so influential in the UK. Ireland was able to adopt a much more low-key approach until the Kilkenny Inquiry of 1993 (Ferguson, 1993). French responses to children at risk are controlled by Juges des Enfants, who normally seek to act supportively towards parents, though they have been criticised for siding more with parents than with children (Foster, 1994).

Models of family policy

As in most areas of economic and social activity, governments tend to lie along a spectrum from interventionist to non-interventionist in family matters. Non-interventionist policies have usually also been 'normalising' in that they have supported conventional family forms with married parents and the male as chief breadwinner, whereas interventionist governments have given more assistance to non-traditional households headed by dual workers, unmarried partners or lone parents. The prominence in the Irish constitution accorded to the autonomy of the family and the special position of the Church has meant that governments there have been very reluctant to confer rights or provide services which appear contrary to parental or religious authority. A primary role for women as homemakers is embodied in the constitution (McLaughlin, 1993). There has been strong resistance to making abortion or divorce legal. It has been pointed out that this policy aims to protects 'the family' within marriage, but leaves largely unprotected those families which are outside marriage or those individuals who suffer within it (Burke, 1991). An extreme example concerned a 14-year old, who was suicidal after being raped and made pregnant. Since all abortions were illegal, she had to travel to the UK for a termination (Lorenz, 1994). The development of Childline services was opposed for a long time, because these were seen as subverting children's loyalties to their parents. Nevertheless, shifting public pressure did bring about some new measures in Ireland during the 1980s, such as the abolition of the status of illegitimacy and creation of a Lone Parents Allowance. Greece is another country where family privacy and parental authority are dominant principles, so that the state has a minimal role both in service provision and in child protection (Hollows and Armstrong, 1991). By contrast Sweden has supported choice and diversity of family forms, for example by giving cohabiting couples similar rights to those who are married and by providing financial and service support so that men and women have equal access to work. This is not simply a matter of religious tradition, since 'Catholic' Italy has also had equal opportunities legislation since the 1970s and permits both divorce and abortion (Ferrara, 1989).

Several countries have attempted to integrate responsibility for all family policies, but in different ways. The first to set up a special ministry was Norway in 1956. This evolved into a Ministry of Children and the Family (Leira, 1993). In Luxembourg the Ministry of the Family has an interesting conglomeration of responsibilities – for social security, preventive services, marital and family counselling, equal opportunities, immigration, refugees and family recreation (Hartmann-Hirsch et al., 1992). Some other countries like Italy have a Family Division within a more general ministry, whilst in 1994 the Secretary of State for Health in the UK was given a general responsibility for 'The Family'.

The idea of having a separate Department for family affairs is superficially attractive, but in practice such ministries have tended to be weak, since they lacked resources, status and clearly defined areas of responsibility (Hill, 1988). An alternative approach intended to overcome this problem of marginalisation has been to oblige all parts of government to take cognizance of family needs. To stand any chance of being effective rather than nominal, this needs to happen alongside explicit family policy goals, coordinating machinery and monitoring procedures. Austria, the Netherlands and Spain have set up a Family Council or Centre. Their functions include:

- seeking to ensure that government departments take account of family interests
- proposing family-oriented policies
- providing a channel of communication between government and non-governmental family organisations.

Again there are dangers that these bodies lack teeth. Another mechanism is to have Family Impact Statements whereby all policy initiatives are obliged to include projections of their implications for family life. These have been quite widely used in North America but have been less popular in Europe.

Kamerman and Kahn (1981) introduced the concept of service-finance packages to describe the differing combinations of ways in which governments choose to intervene in order to affect family income and well-being. Thus a government can select one or more of several different ways to assist with the costs of child care for young children. These include paying parents an allowance, giving parents tax relief, providing low-cost services or subsidising non-governmental agencies who run facilities. Services which make it easier for parents to do paid work can benefit a family financially as much as or more than direct monetary transfers. Subsidies for health care or housing can likewise affect standards of living indirectly. Bradshaw et al. (1993) compared national levels of child support for different types of family, taking account of the influence of employment status and taxation, as well as health, education, housing and day care costs. Belgium, Luxembourg, France and Norway made the highest payments to couples in general, though Germany and the UK do well in relation to low income families. The UK is comparatively generous to lone parents on benefit, whilst Norway, France and Luxembourg ranked highest for lone parents in paid employment.

Sweden was not included in the study, but there the differential in incomes between lone parent and two parent households is amongst the smallest in the world, even though there is no guaranteed income. This results mainly from the high employment rate of lone mothers made possible by extensive day care provision and also in part from the advanced maintenance system following divorce and separation (Duskin, 1990; Ginsburg, 1993). By contrast, limited day care provision, poor employment opportunities and low benefit levels mean that in the UK and Germany many more lone parents rely on the state for income and are living in poverty (Roll, 1991; Ginsburg, 1992).

By bringing together evidence about family policy aims, approaches and particular cash-service combinations, it is possible to identify four main models of family policy in Western Europe, although there are inevitably overlaps:

- *Scandinavian countries* – emphasise citizens' rights to public welfare and gender equality. Policies include parental leave with nearly full wage compensation and widely available high quality day care.
- *The European Union Heartland* – have explicit family policies favouring support to children and parental responsibility, especially taking the form of generous financial allowances and range of multi-purpose early years facilities.
- *The UK and Switzerland* – put greater reliance on implicit family policies and a more residual approach to family support, including comparatively small family allowances and mostly part-time pre-school provision.
- *Ireland and Mediterranean Europe* – many services are provided by religious organisations and there is limited financial support available to families.

Of course these distinctions are not rigid and can change over time. Besides explicit and implicit values about families, many factors have been identified which affect long run differences in the degree and nature of government intervention in social policy (Esping-Anderson, 1990; Lane and Ersson, 1994). These include:

- level of economic development
- extent of urbanisation and influence of rural parties
- social cleavages, especially according to class, region and religious affiliation

- relative influence of left-wing parties and trade unions on government policies
- centralised-federal-decentralised systems
- existence or absence of corporatist approaches to decision-making.

The rest of the chapter examines in more detail some national differences in particular family policy areas, then gives a brief summary of international developments within the European Union.

Variations in financial support to families

Space does not permit detailed consideration of all social security payments affecting families, so I shall concentrate on just a few examples, beginning with the equivalents to child benefit or family allowances. Virtually all West European countries have a universal payment for children, although these were only introduced in Spain in 1991. The schemes differ widely in amount and form, influenced by a mixture of principles and expediency. Thus some favour larger families, whilst different account is taken of lone parenthood, age and birth order. The most generous overall are to be found in Belgium and Luxembourg, with Norway, France and the Netherlands also making high payments (Bradshaw et al., 1993). French *allocations familiales* per child are equivalent to about 10% of the average wage. In Switzerland, proposals for a national scheme of family allowances came up against the strong tradition of local autonomy, with the result that allowances remained the responsibility of each canton, paid at markedly different rates (Tschudi, 1985).

There is no consistency in the ways in which different countries take account of a child's age. In some countries family allowances are higher when children become older because of the supposed higher costs of feeding and clothing bigger children (e.g. Benelux), but elsewhere payments are higher for younger children, as in Norway, on the grounds that the mother is less likely to have paid employment. Yet a third option is to have a flat rate which does not vary with age (e.g. Portugal, Sweden, UK).

Birth order can also affect payments, but in opposite ways since sometimes higher amounts are paid for first borns and sometimes for later borns. In France, payments are made only for second and subsequent children. Originally the British family allowance too was not paid for first borns at all, since it was thought that most parents could and should afford to cover the costs of their first child. Subsequently, the renamed Child Benefit became payable for first children. Later, when the government was under pressure to increase levels after a freeze but did not wish to raise expenditure on every child, the payment for a first child was raised above the rate for subsequent children (Brown, 1992). On the other hand,

Germany and Greece both pay a higher rate for later born children. The child allowances in Germany are paid at a fixed rate for the first child and then, depending on income, at a higher rate for subsequent children (Hantrais, 1994a).

In several countries including the UK, lone parents receive an additional payment. As a result of its wish to encourage the birth rate, France also gives an extra cash grant for any child under 3 and a parental allowance to families with 3 or more children (Baker, 1994). This policy recognises that larger families and those with very young children are least likely to have two adult wage-earners.

Family allowances are often funded mainly by employers (e.g. Belgium, Italy) or through a mixture of employer and employee contributions (Mediterranean Europe). This reflects their origins as rights for workers' families which were then extended to other citizens (Hantrais, 1994b). French allowances are paid by non-governmental Caisses d'Allocations Familiales, funded from a social security budget (with employers contributions) and run by a board with employers' and trade union representatives (Grignon, 1993). Elsewhere the universal basis for allowances is demonstrated in their funding from taxation (UK, Denmark, Netherlands). Several countries have introduced means-testing for their family allowances, partly to save money and partly to target poorer families. This is the case in Italy and Germany (Donati, 1985; Ginsburg, 1992), but so far the UK has resisted this trend.

The means of paying allowances reflect assumptions about cash flow timing and about the distribution of power and money within the family. British parents are unusual in that they may cash payments weekly, whereas elsewhere the money is received monthly or even quarterly. Usually levels of benefit are indexed to take account of inflation and where this has not happened the value has been considerably eroded, as in Germany. In the UK, it has been seen as vital that mothers have access to child benefit since they are more likely to ensure that it is spent on the children. For some poor families, this weekly income is vital for buying necessities (Pahl, 1989). However, the main recipients in Germany are fathers. Belgium regards the payment as more for the child than the parent, so that the allowance is disregarded for the purposes of means-tested family benefits (Schiewe, 1994).

Most countries in Western Europe have tax allowances for children, although not Denmark, the Netherlands or UK. These are regressive measures, in that those with higher earnings benefit most, which was one of the reasons for their abolition in this country. In Germany and Italy more than half of the amount of 'horizontal' financial redistribution to families with children comes through tax relief and half through allowances. Ireland and Spain have substantial allowances for 'dependent' spouses, which is in effect a subsidy for staying home to look after children (Bradshaw et al., 1993).

Financial arrangements for maternal or parental leave are extremely diverse as regards duration, eligibility and amount of replacement income. The UK has a comparatively long period for leave around childbirth, but this is confined to mothers and not well remunerated. Parental leave is available throughout Scandinavia. In 1992, Denmark, Belgium and Germany were the countries in the EC with longest entitlements and highest payments (Dumon, 1992). Danish parents may take leave and receive 90% of their earnings. France has a long period of entitlement, but this is mostly unpaid (Melhuish and Moss, 1991). Differing perceptions of the purpose of maternal or parental leave help account for these divergences. It may be seen as primarily a measure for gender equality (Sweden), for mothers to return quickly to work (France) or for mothers to stay home with children (Germany).

Initially confined to the period around childbirth, parental leave rights have been extended to cover child sickness in several countries. In Norway the entitlement is for 10 days per year, or 20 for lone parents (Leira, 1993). Swedish parents with young children are also entitled to work shorter hours. Pressure to reduce the working hours of both parents has been strong in Denmark, too. Spain and Portugal offer entitlements for parents to work part-time, but in practice low incomes and precarious employment contracts have resulted in low take-up (Moss, 1988).

The high levels of divorce experienced in many places since the 1960s (rising to one in two marriages in Sweden) has meant that states have become increasingly vexed by the issue of ensuring that divorce does not result in child poverty or place excessive financial burdens on the community at large. This has led to the setting up of the controversial Child Support Agency in Britain, modelled largely on arrangements in Australia and the US.

Somewhat different mechanisms are used in other European countries. Dutch child protection agencies take responsibility for pursuing separated parents for child support payments, as do welfare agencies in Austria and Germany which are automatically appointed as guardians to children born outside marriage (Kahn and Kamerman, 1988). The French *allocation de parent isolé* is intended to ensure a basic living income for all lone parent households, including those resulting from divorce or separation, but it is means tested and mainly confined to those with children aged under 3 (Roll, 1991).

In Scandinavia, systems based on standard rates of payment are long established. Whether or not the separated parent contributes, an 'advanced maintenance' is paid by the government to protect children from poverty. It is up to the public authorities to reclaim the money and they have achieved high rates of compliance (80-90%). The Swedish system appears to avoid some of the problems encountered by the British CSA in balancing the needs and responsibilities of original and new families (Bradley, 1990; Ginsburg, 1993). The law was reformed in 1978 against a background of a strong state commitment to redistributing resources in favour of families with children and in minimising gender inequalities resulting from family separation. The old system had been seen as pressing the paying parent too hard in many instances. The new law restricted the obligation to children under 18 in most circumstances and introduced a standard formula for calculating child support based both on the child's needs and the parents resources. In addition a social security benefit (maintenance advance) has been in existence since the 1930s, which guarantees a minimum level of income to support a child with one parent absent. Entitlement is not confined to social security claimants (Kahn and Kamerman, 1988).

Denmark has a long but different tradition of dealing with divorce informally outside the court system by means of the Amtmand (representative of the counties or Amter). These officials handle over 90% of all divorce and separation cases. All parents have a responsibility to support their children financially. The amount is decided by the Amtmand following representations by both parties who also offers mediation concerning access to children. Any shortfall in payment is covered by the social security system, which then assumes responsibility for collection. The authorities obtain nearly 90% of the amounts due.

Variations in early years provision

The age at which compulsory education starts is usually 6 or 7 in continental Europe, but is $4^{1}/_{2}$ to 5 for the UK, Luxembourg and the Netherlands. Day care and educational services for preschool children have been integrated for many years in Scandinavia, the Benelux countries, France and Germany. This contrasts with the recent and piecemeal trend towards combined centres in the UK. The numbers of places available in early years centres (adjusted for population differences) are generally much higher than in the UK or Southern Europe. Over 90% of 3-4 year olds attend a centre in Belgium and France (Glasner, 1992). Opening hours are also generally longer than has been common in British nursery schools, which makes life easier for working parents. Nevertheless, only a few countries (notably Denmark) have widespread group care for children under 3, though France has substantial numbers of children aged 2 attending nursery schools (Melhuish and Moss, 1991).

Sweden, Denmark, Belgium and France have open access to public facilities which is largely based on demand, since the services are seen as primarily intended to enable parents to work and to furnish high quality socialisation for children. Elsewhere places are often restricted to 'priority categories' such as poor families or lone parent families. This applies to Portugal, Luxembourg and the UK (Council of Europe, 1988). In both Sweden and France employers' social insurance contributions help cover the cost of neighbourhood provision (cf. the limited tax concessions for work based nurseries in the UK). The UK represents a middle position in terms of the pluralism of providers, which ranges from nearly all local authority in Sweden to almost completely voluntary and private in Ireland.

Most countries have moved away from separate facilities for disabled children except for Greece. Integration is particularly advanced in Catalonia and Emilia-Romagna. Segregated provision for ethnic minority children exists in some places. Many facilities disregard ethnic background, but countries like Germany and the Netherlands have pursued multicultural approaches which acknowledge and respect cultural differences. Anti-racist child care is uncommon outside the UK (Moss, 1988).

There are extensive organised childminding schemes in France, Portugal and Belgium (Moss, 1990). Belgium has subsidised 'reception families' who provide full-time day care and after school care. These are linked to day care centres and parents make a financial contribution according to their income (Mostinckx, 1992). Swiss organisations encourage close co-operation and regular meetings of parents and childminders (Council of Europe, 1988). In 1992, France introduced a cash benefit for those employing childminders (Grignon, 1993). Several other countries give tax relief for day care costs.

The expansion of services in Scandinavia to approach demand came later than in countries like Belgium and France. Sweden expanded day care rapidly from a low base in the 1970s and 1980s. All approved centres are given state subsidies and are well resourced. As in Denmark, priority is given to mothers working full-time, but equally strong emphasis is placed on the development of the child.

Partly cause and partly effect, the employment rates of women are usually higher in those countries with more extensive early years provision. For example nearly half of mothers with young children are employed full-time in Denmark, roughly five times the British rate (Moss 1990). Similarly, a far higher proportion of lone parents work.

Services for children at risk or away from home

The organisation and auspices for public child welfare services are quite diverse. Mostly these are run by local government (e.g. Belgium, Denmark), but in France a mixture of professionals working for the communes, departments and quasi-autonomous bodies operate from the same building (Cannan et al., 1992; Daines, 1993). Family services in both the Republic of Ireland and Northern Ireland are part of central government health boards (Gilligan, 1991: Warner, 1993). There has been a common trend for child welfare services to be decentralised (Pijl, 1993). Social workers often work alongside or under the direction of health or legal professionals.

In most countries voluntary agencies play a major role in both prevention and substitute care (Cannan et al., 1992; Gilligan, 1991). Dutch services are mainly provided by a wide range of private and voluntary bodies, although most of these have substantial public funding, often 100%. This stems from the country's religious pluralism and a strong tradition of 'pillarisation', in which welfare functions are distributed amongst several 'pillars' or groupings in society (Pijl, 1993). Generally, the links between education and social work are close on the Continent, where there is a distinct intermediate profession of pedagogy (Lorenz, 1994). In France, recreational and training schemes appear to have been successful in diverting young people from delinquency (King, 1988).

Increasingly in the UK, access to services has become conditional on formal assessment and registration of risk (Gibbons, Ch. 6 this volume). Elsewhere there is still a much stronger emphasis on availability of support according to demand and on a voluntary basis. Barth (1992) observed that, by contrast with the United States, 'child abuse or neglect is not a necessary or even typical precondition to beginning child welfare services' in Sweden. Even when there are professional concerns about the quality of care, the approach to child protection in the Netherlands is much more based on cooperation and counselling than the legalistic response which has come to characterise British responses to alleged child abuse (Christopherson, 1989). According to Armstrong and Hollows (1991), the Dutch Confidential Doctor system 'provides a widely accessible, low threshold access to facilities' (p. 147). In Germany and Belgium too multi-disciplinary centres offering therapeutic work have become common. In France, on the other hand, the legal system is normally involved at an early stage, but the 'Juges des Enfants' operate in an informal participatory manner with an emphasis on helping families to function better. As in Scotland, child protection and juvenile justice are dealt with in the same non-adversarial system. There are still tensions around issues of trust and risk, but the investigative and decision-making roles of the Juge to some extent allow social workers to work more closely and therapeutically with families (Cooper, 1994; Hetherington, 1994).

Large residential institutions still exist in a number of countries. Residential nurseries for infants and young children with a primarily medical orientation have now virtually disappeared in the UK but can still be found in France (Ely and Saunders, 1992). However the general trend has been towards units of smaller size, against a background of declining overall numbers in residential establishments (Colton and Hellinckx,

1993). In many parts of Italy, large religious institutions have been replaced by family group homes (Gugliemetti and Sapucci, 1991). Another trend has been the professionalisation of residential staff. In the Low Countries, units are mainly run by group workers and carers with an educational (social pedagogic) background (Crimmens, 1994).

The comparative decline in residential care has been associated with a growth in foster care in some countries, but not in others where the development of home-based services seems to have been more critical (Madge, 1994). Sweden pioneered the creation of specialist fostering schemes for adolescents (Hazel, 1991). Some countries with no tradition of non-kin fostering have only recently and with difficulty managed to recruit significant numbers of foster carers. This is true of Spain, where only one in ten children accommodated away from home are fostered (Colton and Hellinckx, 1993).

Most countries have developed services to support children at home and so to reduce the need for reception into care. For instance, in Ireland Child Care Workers and Home Helps provide a range of counselling, educational, befriending and practical assistance (Kavanagh, 1992). Innovatory schemes include working with family social networks in Sweden and intensive multi-disciplinary work with the under-twelves in the Netherlands. Video home training is another Dutch initiative, which helps parents learn and improve skills in dealing with their children (Madge, 1994). The Netherlands also has Youth Advisory Centres which offer advice and advocacy for young people with personal and practical difficulties, especially those who have run away from home or residential care (Pijl, 1992). Several countries have developed flexi-care and shared care arrangements whereby children spend part or most of their time at home and part in care, e.g. for week-end breaks in Denmark and Ireland. Family services are less developed in Mediterranean countries or else have quite specialised functions, like family planning in Spain (Casado, 1992).

Internationalisation of family support

Actions by governments are becoming increasingly influenced by international agreements, such as the UN Convention on Children's Rights; pan-European agreements about adoption; and Council of Europe policies on day care and youth. However, undoubtedly one of the most important developments has been the growing role of the the European Community (now European Union).

Unlike national governments, the EU does not itself provide services or finance directly to families. The original European *Economic* Community was established primarily with economic and political aims. Only gradually and tentatively has it taken limited steps in the social policy sphere and even then mostly as a by-product of labour market and regional measures largely aimed at improving employment opportunities. In particular there are Structural and Cohesion Funds set up to counterbalance economic and regional inequalities. However this finance has been tapped by both voluntary agencies and local government to create small scale but locally significant facilities for families, usually as part of employment creation or training schemes. For instance, one of the projects set up under the Third Poverty Action Programme was a multi-purpose self-help centre for lone parents in Bristol. European Social Fund money has been used for training and short-term employment in a number of pre-school and family centre projects in Scotland (see also Long, Ch. 4). Young people can also participate in educational exchanges through EU schemes.

A more extensive influence of the European Union in the field of family policy has been exerted through two other mechanisms – legislation and networking. These have mostly been directed towards the family entitlements of migrant workers and employment opportunities for women, though with increasing recognition of the importance of related measures like parental leave and child care provision which support families in optimising the socialisation of children.

Legislative measures have established rights for both workers and their families who have migrated within the Union to receive social security if they become ill or unemployed (Baldwin-Edwards, 1991). Likewise they are entitled to child benefit or its equivalent in the host country. France used to pay allowances at the rate of the family's home country (which were nearly always lower), but since a European Court judgment in 1989 it has been obliged to pay at the French rate.

Since its inception, the EC was committed by the Treaty of Rome to gender equality in relation to paid employment (Szyszczak, 1987). Directives passed in the 1970s gave women and men rights to equal pay, equal access to employment and training and equal treatment in social security matters. Test cases in the European Court of Justice have obliged governments to bring their own legislation into line with these directives (Steiner, 1988). For instance the Court has established that it is unlawful to refuse employment to pregnant women or to give part-time workers longer probationary periods than full-time workers. EC laws passed during the 1980s increased women's rights to occupational benefits and extended equal opportunities rights to self-employed women. These changes were included in the UK 1989 Social Security Act. However, proposals to make paid parental leave available in all member states did not come to fruition. The European Commission's White Paper on 'European Social Policy' (CEC, 1994) proposed further measures to address stereotyped roles and to establish a baseline infrastructure of child care services.

Besides its legislative action, the EC has also fostered various projects, networks, seminars and conferences to further the interests of women, mainly as regards training and employment. The Second Action programme on the Promotion of Equal Opportunities for Women lobbied for expanded child care provision. It set up a Network on Child Care whose activities include compiling comparative data about the needs for day care and the services available (Moss, 1990). The Network has argued that the provision of uniform high quality day care in all EU countries is a requirement of the Single Market, since otherwise women with children will be disadvantaged with respect of free movement of labour.

Only during the 1980s did the European Community begin to express explicit family policy aims which are broader than gender equality in employment. In 1983 the European Parliament (admittedly the weakest of the EC institutions) stated that family policy should become an integral part of all Community policies. The Commission sponsored meetings for ministers with responsibility for family affairs and set up the European Observatory on Family Policies consisting of 12 national experts to monitor family trends and policies (Hantrais 1994b).

The Commission has also assisted in the development of a Confederation of Family Organisations in the European Community (COFACE). This acts as a coordinating, information-sharing and lobbying body in relation to family aspects of EU policy. It represents an international network linking different welfare sectors – formal governmental organisations, voluntary bodies, academic institutions consumer groups. COFACE supports policies which improve the work-family interface e.g. through after-school care; part-time working with full social protection. One of its aims is to improve the harmonisation and co-ordination of national policies (e.g. as regards schooling) to make it easier for families who move from one country to another.

Conclusions

Nearly all the countries of Western Europe have developed policies to support families which are more interventionist than is the case amongst countries with comparable or higher standards of living in North America or on the Pacific Rim (Jones, 1993). In spite of the near universal retrenchment in welfare states experienced during the 1980s, family policy issues have usually managed to maintain or even strengthen their position. This has been in part due to the influence of women's movements and changing employment patterns, especially in Northern Europe. There has also been a tendency to disaggregate 'the family', with a recognition that the interests of children, women and men sometimes coincide, but sometimes diverge or conflict. A further dimension of change has been the increased internationalisation of awareness and influences. This is illustrated by the development of family policies within the European Union, the implementation and monitoring of the UN Convention on the Rights of the Child and such events as the International Year of the Family in 1994.

As experience of the Child Support Agency illustrated, it is rarely wise to import ideas from abroad without careful preparation and adjustment to the local circumstances. However, comparisons with other countries and the small but growing international influence on domestic family policy can stimulate critical evaluation of support systems for families in the UK.

References

Baker, J. (1986) 'Comparing national priorities: Family and population policy in Britain and France' *Journal of Social Policy*, 15, 4, 421-442.

Baker, J. (1994) 'Social protection in France: history and prospects for the 1990s', in R. Page and J. Baldock (eds.) (1994) *Social Policy Review 6*. Canterbury: Social Policy Assocation.

Baldwin-Edwards, M. (1991) 'The socio-political rights of migrants in the European Community', in Room, G. (ed.) *Towards a European Welfare State*. Bristol: SAUS Publications.

Barth, R. P. (1992) 'Child welfare services in the United States and Sweden: different assumptions, laws and outcomes', *Scandinavian Journal of Social Welfare*, 1, 36-42.

Bradley, D. (1990) 'Financial support for children – The Swedish example' *Family Law*, 349-350.

Bradshaw, J., Ditch, J. Holmes, H. and Whiteford, P. (1993) *Support for Children: A Comparison of Arrangements in Fifteen Countries*. York: Social Policy Research Unit.

Brown J. C. (1992) 'Which way for the family: choices for the 1990s', in N. Manning and R. page (eds.) *Social Policy Review 4*. London: Social Policy Assn.

Burke, H. (1991) 'Changing demography, changing needs and unprotected families', in Keily, G. and Richardson, V. (eds.) *Family Policy: European Perspectives*. Dublin: Family Studies Centre.

Cannan, C., Berry, L. and Lyons, K. (1992) *Social Work and Europe*. London: Macmillan.

Casado, D. (1992) 'Spain' in Munday, B. (ed.) *Social Services in the Member States of the European Community: A Handbook of Information and Data*. Canterbury: European Institute of Social Services.

Christopherson, J. (1989) 'European child-abuse management systems', in O. Stevenson (ed.) *Child Abuse: Professional Practice and Public Policy*. London: Harvester Wheatsheaf.

Colton, M. and Hellinckx, W. (eds.) (1993) *Child Care in the EC*. Cambridge: Arena.

Commission of the European Communities (C.E.C.) (1994) *European Social Policy – A Way Forward for the Union*. Luxembourg: Commission of the European Communities.

Cooper, A. (194) 'In care or en famille? Child protection, the family and the state in France and England', *Social Work in Europe*, 1, 1, 59-67.

Council of Europe (1988) *Forms of Child Care*. Strasbourg: Council of Europe.

Crimmens, D. (1994) 'Residential Childcare: The future of comparative European research' *Social Work in Europe*, 1, 1, 22–26.

Daines, R. (1993) *Bridging the Channel: Practice Teaching in France and the United Kingdom*, London: CCETSW.

Deakin, N. (1988) 'Family and Government'. In *Families and the State*. London: Family Policy Studies Centre.

Dominelli, L. (1991) *Women Across Continents: Feminist Comparative Social Policy*. Hemel Hempstead: Harvester Wheatsheaf.

Donati, P. (1985) 'Social welfare and social services in Italy since 1950', in Girod, R. Laubier, P. de, and Gladstone, A. (eds.) *Social Policy in Western Europe and the USA, 1950–1980*. London: Macmillan.

Dumon, W. (1992) *Family Policy in the EEC Countries*. Luxembourg: Commission of the European Communities.

Duskin, E. (ed.) (1990) *Lone Parent Families*. Paris: OECD.

Ely, P. and Saunders, R. (1992) 'France' in Munday, B. (ed.) *Social Services in the Member States of the European Community: A Handbook of Information and Data*. Canterbury: European Institute of Social Services.

Esping-Andersen, G. (1990) *The Three Worlds of Welfare Capitalism*. Princeton: Princeton University Press.

Ferrara, M. (1989) 'Italy', in Dixon, J. and Scheurell, R. P. (eds.) *Social Welfare in Developed Market Countries*. London: Routledge.

Ferguson, H. (1993) 'The manifest and latent implications of the report of the Kilkenny Incest Investigation for social work', *Irish Social Worker*, 11, 4, 4–5.

Ford, R. and Chakrabarti, M. (eds.) (1987) *Welfare Abroad*. Edinburgh: Scottish Academic Press.

Foster, M-C. (1994) 'The Juge des Enfants and child protection in France', *Children & Society*, 8, 3, 200–213.

Gilligan, R. (1991) *Irish Child Care Services*, Dublin: Institute of Public Administration.

Ginsburg, N. (1992) *Divisions of Welfare: A Critical Approach to Comparative Social Policy*. London: Sage.

Ginsburg, N. (1993) 'Sweden: The Social-Democratic Case', in A. Cochrane and J. Clarke (eds.) *Comparing Welfare States*. London: Sage.

Girod, R. Laubier, P. de, and Gladstone, A. (eds.) (1985) *Social Policy in Western Europe and the USA, 1950–1980*. London: Macmillan.

Glasner, A. (1992) 'Gender and Europe: cultural and structural impediments to change', in J. Bailey (ed.) *Social Europe*. London: Longman.

Gottesman, M. (ed.) *Residential Child Care: An International Reader*. London: Whiting and Birch.

Grignon, M. (1993) 'Conceptualising French family policy: the social actors', in Hantrais, L. and Mangen, S. (eds.) *The Policy Making Process and the Social Actors*. Loughborough: Cross-National Research Group.

Gugliemetti, F. and Sapucci, G. (1991) 'Residential education in Italy', in M. Gottesman (ed.) *Residential Child Care: An International Reader*. London: Whiting and Birch.

Hantrais, L. (1994) 'Comparing family policy in Britain, France and Germany', *Journal of Social Policy*, 23, 2, 135–160.

Hantrais, L. (1994b) 'Family policy in Europe', in R. Page and J. Baldock (eds.) (1994) *Social Policy Review 6*, Canterbury: Social Policy Assocation.

Hartmann-Hirsch, M., Welter, C. and Neyens, M. (1992) 'The Grand Duchy of Luxembourg' in Munday, B. (ed.) *Social Services in the Member States of the European*

Community: *A Handbook of Information and Data*. Canterbury: European Institute of Social Services.

Hazel, N. (1991) 'The development of specialist foster care for adolescents: Policy and practice', in Galaway, B., Maglajlic, D., Husdon, J., Harmon, P. and McLagan, J. (eds.) *International Perspectives on Specialist Foster Family Care*. St Paul: Human Services Associates.

Hetherington, R. (1994) 'Trans-Manche partnerships', *Adoption & Fostering* 18, 3, 17–20.

Hill, M. (1988) *Towards a Family Policy?* Edinburgh, SCAFA.

Hollows, A. and Armstrong, H. (1991) 'Responses to child abuse in the EC' in M. Hill (ed.) *Social Work and the European Community*. London: Jessica Kingsley.

Jones, C. (1985) *Patterns of Social Policy*. London: Tavistock.

Jones, C. (ed.) 1993) *New Perspectives on the Welfare State in Europe*. London: Routledge.

Kamerman, S. and Kahn, A. J. (1981) *Child Care, Family Benefits and Working Parents*. Columbia University Press, New York.

Kamerman, S. and Kahn, A. J. (1987) *Mothers Alone*. New York: Auburn House.

Kahn, A. J. and Kamerman, S. B. (1988) *Child Support*. Beverley Hills: Sage.

Kamerman, S. and Kahn, A. J. (1992) *Child Care, Parental Leave and the Under 3s*. New York: Auburn House.

Kavanagh, L. (1992) 'Republic of Ireland' in Munday, B. (ed.) *Social Services in the Member States of the European Community: A Handbook of Information and Data*. Canterbury: European Institute of Social Services.

King, M. (1988) *How to Make Crime Prevention Work*. London: NACRO.

Land, H. and Parker, R. (1978) 'Family Policy in the United Kingdom', in S. Kamerman and A. J. Kahn (eds.) *Family Policy Government and Families in Fourteen Countries*. New York: Columbia University Press.

Lane, J-E and Ersson, S. O. (1994) *Politics and Society in Western Europe*. London: Sage.

Leira, A. (1993) 'Mothers, markets and the State: A Scandinavian model?', *Journal of Social Policy*, 22, 3, 329–348.

Lorenz, W. (1994) *Social Work in a Changing Europe*. London: Routledge.

McLaughlin, E. (1993) 'Ireland: Catholic Corporatism', in A. Cochrane and J. Clarke (eds.) *Comparing Welfare States*. London: Sage.

Macnicol, J. (1978) 'Family allowances and less eligibility', in P. Thane (ed.) *The Origins of British Social Policy*. London: Croom Helm.

Madge, N. (1994) *Children and Residential Care in Europe*. London: National Children's Bureau.

Melhuish, E. C. and Moss, P. (1991) *Day Care for Younger Children: International Prespectives*. London: Routledge.

Moss, P. (1988) *Child Care and Equality of Opportunity*. Brussels: Commission of the European Communities.

Moss, P. (1990) 'Childcare and equality of opportunity', in L. Hantrais, S. Mangen and M. O'Brien (eds.) *Caring and the Welfare state in the 1990s*. Loughborough: Cross-National Research Group.

Mostinckx, J. (1992) 'The Flemish Community of Belgium', in Munday, B. (ed.) *Social Services in the Member States of the European Community: A Handbook of Information and Data*. Canterbury: European Institute of Social Services.

Munz, R. and Wintersberger, H. (1987) 'The making of the Austrian welfare state', in R. Friedmann, N. Gilbert and M. Sherer (eds.) *Modern Welfare States*. Brighton: Wheatsheaf.

Olsson, S. and McMurphy, S. (1993) 'Social policy in Sweden: The Swedish model in transition', in R. Page and J. Baldock (eds.) *Social Policy Review 5*. Canterbury: Social Policy Association.

Pahl, J. (1989) *Money and Marriage*. London: Macmillan.

Pijl, M. A. (1992) 'Information on Social Services in the Netherlands', in Munday, B. (ed.) *Social Services in the Member States of the European Community: A Handbook of Information and Data*. Canterbury: European Institute of Social Services.

Pijl, M. A. (1993) 'The Dutch welfare state: a product of relgious and political pluralism' in R. Page and J. Baldock (eds.) *Social Policy Review 5*. Canterbury: Social Policy Association.

Roll, J. (1991) 'One in ten: lone parent families in the European Community', in N. Manning (ed.) *Social Policy Review 1990–91*. London, Longman.

Schiewe, K. (1994) 'Labour marker, welfare state and family institutions', *Journal of European Social Policy*, 4, 3, 201–224.

Siim, B. (1990) 'Women and the welfare state: Between private and public dependence. A comparative approach to care work in Denmark and Britain', in C. Ungerson (ed.) *Gender and Caring: Work and Welfare in Britain and Scandinavia*. Hemel Hempstead: Harvester Wheatsheaf.

Steiner, J. (1988) *Textbook on EEC Law*. London: Blackstone Press.

Szyszczak, E. (1987) 'The future of women's rights: the role of European Community Law' in M. Brenton and C. Ungerson (eds.) *Yearbook of Social Policy 1986–7*. London: Longman.

Tizard, J., Moss, P. and Perry, J. (1976) *All our Children*. London: Temple Smith.

Triseliotis, J. (1994) 'The legacy of the past on systems of care for separated children', in Asquith, S. and Hill, M. (eds.) *Justice for Children*. Dordrecht: Martinus Nijhoff.

Tschudi, H-P. (1985) 'Swiss social policy since 1950', in Girod, R. Laubier, P. de, and Gladstone, A. (eds.) *Social Policy in Western Europe and the USA, 1950–1980*. London: Macmillan.

Vedel-Petersen, J. (1991) 'Families with young children: the situation in Denmark' in M. Hill (ed.) *Social Work and the European Community*. London: Jessica Kingsley.

Warner, N. (1993) 'Information on Social Services in Northern Ireland', in Munday, B. (ed.) *Social Services in the Member States of the European Community: A Handbook of Information and Data*. Canterbury: European Institute of Social Services.

3

CHANGING FAMILIES
Martin Richards

Introduction

THERE is a general view that we are in the middle of a period of very rapid change in family life. Then a widespread reaction to this is to condemn the changes and to suggest we should resist them. However, it is not always clear exactly what the changes are that are being condemned or indeed how they might be resisted. Indeed, much of the reaction seems rather more an expression of disquiet and discomfort in an uncertain world rather than anything that might be accurately termed a debate at all. Often the claims are very general – for instance, that family life is in terminal decline. Yet the great majority of the population live in a household they themselves would describe as a family and preserve active links with a wider network of kin. Indeed, a recent survey found that a third of us live within an hour's travel of our family of origin. 11% of adults see our mothers daily while 58% said they phoned or wrote at least once a week (Finch and Mason, 1993).

Another common perception is of 'rocketing' divorce rates. In fact, rates have been rather stable since the late 1970s; albeit there had been a dramatic rise in the decade before that. Two thirds of current marriages are likely to end with a parting caused by death, rather than divorce. And, one might further comment, that a province of the UK (namely, Northern Ireland) has one of the lowest divorce rates in Europe.

But my purpose in this chapter is not to deny or play down change. Change there certainly is. But I want to try and establish more precisely what is happening. What are the significant trends in family life? I will concentrate on issues related to parents and children. My aim is to get at some of the processes that underlie some of the changes. I suggest that it is not only untrue but also quite unhelpful to talk in terms of a general decline in family life. We need to be much more precise before judgements are made; to clarify exactly what it is that is changing and to try to understand why change is taking place. Only then can we begin to think about policies which might reduce change (if change is demonstrably undesirable) or help to relieve some of its undesirable consequences.

We need to examine the current Government ideology of family values against a precise analysis of contemporary family life. This ideology stresses the separation of the 'private' world of the family and the public sphere of the state and the economy. The family is held to be the realm of individual responsibility – where moral values are taught, the young are controlled and supported as they move into adulthood. It is where the sick and aged are supported and largely cared for. Reproduction is to be confined as far as possible to the two parent family and ideally the right to reproduce is removed from all those except heterosexual couples, according to the ideology.

The subject of family life is, of course, a very large one and I have had to restrict my scope in a number of ways. As I have said already my central concern is parents and children. I will not, for instance, address the important issue of the ageing of our society. Nor will I do justice to the ethnic diversity and related diversity of family patterns found in the United Kingdom. In discussing the topic of sexual relations I will restrict what I say to heterosexual relations.

Trends in family life

While most children in the UK are born within marriage, a growing proportion are born to cohabiting couples. Overall about a third of births are to unmarried parents (one fifth in Northern Ireland) and though official statistics do not record the circumstances, it is generally assumed that in the majority of cases these are cohabiting couples since both parents register the birth (See Appendix 1 for a note of sources for statements about family demography).

Britain has experienced a rapid decline in marriage rates (now the lowest since records began in the last century) and a rise in cohabitation. Cohabitation is now the norm before marriage and a majority of those under 45 believe that young people should live together as a prelude to marriage. However, as Kiernan and Estaugh (1993) point out in their recent study, the term cohabitation covers a wide range of situations and living arrangements. Very broadly speaking three groups may be distinguished, young never married childless couples, those previously married and those who have never married and have children. For the first of these groups, cohabitation tends to be short lived and the couple either marry or split up. In terms of their social background and education the study found that these cohabiting couples looked very similar to the young married childless population in general.

The majority popular opinion still holds that people who want children should be married and most still regard cohabitation as a prelude to both marriage and child bearing. When the time for the wedding does come, the occasion is likely to be marked by a larger and more expensive ceremony than was common in the recent past and, for about half of all couples, it will be a religious ceremony despite much lower rates of regular religious observance. In recent years the age at both marriage and the birth of a first child have increased. Average age at a first birth rose from 24.7. in 1961 to 27.7 years in 1991.

Surveys of the sexual behaviour of young people indicate that the average age at first sexual intercourse has declined slightly over recent decades and it seems likely that the number of partners has increased before a young person reaches the point when they cohabit for the first time or marry. It is also probably true that there has been an increase in the average number of cohabiting relationships before marriage. These trends also imply effective fertility control as the proportion of births outside marriage born to teenage mothers has decreased sharply over the past 20 years.

Not surprisingly, couples involved in the second type of cohabitation – those who have been previously married – tend to be older and in about half the cases have children from an earlier marriage. Like the premarital cohabitations there is very little to distinguish this group in social terms from the equivalent married population. In contrast to these first two groups, the final group – the never-married couples with children – are different and are relatively disadvantaged. Compared with their married counterparts this group have lower incomes, are more likely to be in receipt of income supplement and housing benefit, to live in local authority housing and for the male partner to be unemployed or to have a semi-skilled or unskilled job (Kiernan and Estaugh, 1993). To put it in other terms, those who are occupationally and economically less well off are less likely to convert their cohabitation into a marriage before they begin child-bearing.

In the European context our experience of cohabitation and births to unmarried couples is very much the middle of the road. Over the past decade a rise in extra-marital births has been more or less general throughout Europe (cohabitation is much harder to quantify). Rates remain low in Southern Europe (less than 10% in Spain, Italy, Switzerland and Greece, for example) while in most of the Nordic countries births *within* marriage have become the minority. But even in the Nordic countries it would be over-simple to say there is a general rejection of formal marriage. It seems more a case of postponement beyond the start of child-bearing.

In Europe, as elsewhere, there is a great deal of variation between ethnic groups. In Britain, while cohabitation rates are higher amongst black Afro-Caribbean couples than for the white majority, rates are very low indeed for communities of Indian, Pakistani or Bangladeshi origin.

Of course, the situation at the birth of a child may not remain unchanged until the children grow up and leave home. For those born outside marriage many will experience the marriage of their parents and a minority of those with married parents (about 25%) will go through a separation. Rising divorce rates and endings of cohabitations have led to increasing numbers of lone parent households. These make up about a fifth of households with children in the UK (though there is wide geographical and ethnic variation) and the great majority are headed by women. Single parenthood is a less stable category than marriage or cohabitation and for many children this will be but a temporary phase in their lives before it is replaced by stepparenthood whether through a remarriage or cohabitation. Transitions for children are not systematically recorded so it is not possible to give an overall picture of the changing parental relations and household compositions for that minority of children who do not remain with both their parents (whether married or not).

Income and employment

I shall now turn to matters related to income and employment. These are dealt with briefly here as they are discussed more fully elsewhere in the book (See Long, Chapter 4). Often a strong conceptual division is drawn between the 'private' world of the household and the family, and the public sphere of employment, earnings and politics. Indeed, as I have already mentioned, it has become a matter of political ideology over the past decade or so, to discuss family life as if it carried on in a world quite independent from the public and especially economic sphere. While the public world is seen in terms of the needs of the economy, employment and unemployment and the free market, family life has been regarded as a matter of individual choice, personal responsibility and moral values. The maintenance of such a division allows the pursuit of economic policies which damage family life, while at the same time attributing difficulties in the home to the moral and other inadequacies of the individuals involved, as has become a central theme in Government policies. But despite the rhetoric, domestic life does not exist in isolation from the rest of society. It is influenced at all levels by employment, income and the fabric of daily life in the public sphere. While economic factors are not, of course, the sole determinant of patterns of relationships and child rearing, they have a profound effect on domestic life.

In relation to income the overall pattern is clear: over the last decade or so, we find that the rich have become richer and the poor poorer, and that poverty has borne particularly heavily on households with children. Current research suggests that we have now reached the level where a fifth of the nation's children now live in poverty (Oppenheim, 1993).

Using either relative or absolute resource measures, poverty has increased over the past decade (Oppenheim, 1993; Roll, 1992). For example in 1988/89 twelve million people (22% of the population) were living below 50% of average income level (after housing costs) as compared with 9% of the population in 1979. Over this period average incomes rose – by 30% for the population as a whole in real terms. But this average figure conceals a fall in income of 6% for the poorest tenth of the population, while the top tenth had an increase of 46%. The fall for the poorest 10% is largely explained by the rise in unemployment and changes in social security. In terms of children there was a doubling over the decade from 11% to 22% living in poverty. But the situation varies with type of household. In 1989 76% of children living with a lone parent were living in poverty compared with 13% of those with two adults.

Research on resources clearly demonstrates the very significant costs of child rearing (Bradshaw, 1993). Using 1993 prices, it was found that a modest but adequate level required a gross income of £10,175 per annum for a single man and £12,568 for a couple without children. But a household with two children, whether headed by two parents or one, needed over £19,000 per year. Such figures make it very obvious why very low standards of income are the lot for so many lone parent households. Not surprisingly, these trends have had effects on the indicators of health, growth and nutrition of children growing up in different circumstances. Long-term improvements in some of these have slowed in the 1980s and the differences across social class groups have become wider.

In recent decades there have been major changes in patterns of work and unemployment which have had important effects, economically and socially, for households with children. In particular, the proportion of mothers in paid employment has increased, as has unemployment, especially of men. In 1992 the General Household Survey found that 63% of married or cohabiting women with dependent children were in paid work with two thirds working part-time. Increasingly, families owe their standard of living to two incomes. Not only are more mothers in paid work but they are returning to work sooner after childbirth. Over the past twenty years the proportion of mothers of under fives at work has doubled to 50% (about a quarter working full-time). In contrast to these increases, the proportion of lone parent mothers in the labour force was 42% in 1992 and had fallen from a peak of 49% in the 1970s. These changes in the employment of mothers have not been paralleled by a corresponding increase in child care provision at work places.

In this area, as in all the issues I have been discussing, it is important to recognise the variation by region and community. In unemployment, for example, there are rising gradients as one moves north and west of London. But within these broad trends there are particularly high levels in communities which once depended on 'traditional' industries which have now vanished. There is ethnic variation too with higher unemployment, for instance, in the black communities.

The broader picture

It would be possible to collect a huge variety of social, demographic and economic statistics which would indicate changes in family life over the past decades – or indeed over a longer time span. I have described a very few of what I think are the more significant, ones related to the lives of children and their parents. How can we understand these changes? I think we would need to consider four broad areas:

- Marriage and cohabitation
- Child bearing
- Patterns of sexual relations
- Economic policies.

Marriage and cohabitation

While it is often the proportion of children born outside marriage or the numbers of lone parent households that attract attention, the former reflecting the rise in cohabitation and the latter the fragility of marriage, these changes seem to conceal a much more fundamental shift in our society – that in the nature of marriage itself.

The last century or so has seen the development of what has been called companionate marriage (and here I take marriage to include marriage-like cohabitation). Companionate marriage places emphasis on the quality relationship of the partners, as companions and friends, as well as spouses and lovers. It is a form of marriage in which the love relationship is stressed rather than the formal structure of the arrangement. This form of marriage emerged amongst middle class couples in the 19th century and has since become predominant throughout our society (e.g. Reibstein and Richards, 1992).

Placing as it does an emphasis on the quality of the relationship between the spouses, companionate marriage is based on the individual choice of the two partners with little or no involvement of the wider kin. With a nuclear family kinship structure the couple will typically set up a home together at marriage or earlier when they begin a cohabiting relationship. Over the century as the companionate ideal developed, the notion of exclusiveness has emphasised the relationship in the ways a couple is expected to spend their leisure time together, and, particularly, in their expectation of a monogamous sexual relationship. There is direct evidence of increased emphasis on the ideal of monogamy over the post war decades (Elliott and Richards, 1991).

An association can be observed between the historical development of companionate marriage and a rising rate of divorce (Philips, 1988). I have argued elsewhere that these two are causally connected – that companionate marriage, with its emphasis on exclusiveness and the quality of relationship, is inherently unstable and will be associated with a relatively high divorce rate (Richards, 1994). When the relationship does not live up to expectation, the increasing tendency is to try again in a new one, creating a pattern of serial monogamy.

There is also an important issue of gender. The companionate concept embodies the idea of a more or less equally shared domestic life and division of labour in the home. In early stages of the relationship when both partners are likely to be in the labour force, sharing household tasks may prove relatively easy. The coming of children typically leads to an increased sexual division of household labour together with the intrusion of children into the exclusive marriage relationship (Losh-Hesselbant,1987). This seems the likely explanation of the fall in marital satisfaction reported at this time, especially by women. The gender difference may be explained in part by the double burden of paid and domestic work which many women carry, as well as the greater emphasis placed by women on closeness and a shared emotional life (Reibstein and Richards, 1992). Not surprisingly, it is women who most commonly take the first legal step to end a marriage.

There is much discussion of the social isolation of the nuclear family, but research indicates that support between kin is important to many people in contemporary Britain (Finch, 1989). The development of private transport, as well as the phone and post have made contact between kin members living distant from each other easier than ever before. While members of the wider network may play a significant part in rites of passage such as weddings and funerals, most support and notions of duty and obligation exist between kin who have at sometime resided together – i.e. parents, children and siblings. Divorce often fractures kinship relations and may effectively wipe out the otherwise persisting relationship that kin and co-residence may create.

Other factors are also involved in the post war rise in divorce. With rising female employment the financial need for marriage for women has declined. Working mothers are more likely to divorce (Ermisch, 1993). The difficulties of juggling domestic and paid work with child care and the rising expectations of sharing responsibilities with a husband contribute to this trend (Lewis and Cooper, 1988). There are also claims based on social attitude evidence that younger women value autonomy, education and employment more than family life and parenting (Wilkinson, 1994).

Here, as in most matters discussed in this chapter, there are wide differences between ethnic groups. What has just been said relates to English kinship (e.g. Harris, 1990) and may not apply to other groups.

Child bearing and child rearing

Over the past century fertility has declined much in line with the rise in companionate marriage. Once again it is tempting to suggest a connection (see Miller, 1987). Here the link may be because a declining number of children permits the development of a companionate relationship between spouses, but equally that such a relationship encourages the restriction of births. But, of course, we should be cautious of glib and simplistic explanations. Many other factors need to be considered including the decline in infant and childhood mortality (itself providing both a cause and an effect), the rise of State education, changes in the nature of work, and the increasing emphasis on the quality of parental care as a determinant of personality, character and life chances. What can be ruled out as a significant cause is the development of more effective contraceptive methods. There were no important developments in the late 19th century during a period of particular rapid decline in fertility. Indeed, it seems much more plausible to see the development of new methods of contraception and their wider availability as a response to a growing desire to control fertility.

The chances of a child reaching adulthood in a household containing both parents remains much the same as it was in the mid 19th century, but when a parent is absent nowadays it is more often because of separation and divorce, rather than death as it was then. What is historically remarkable is the intervening period when adult death rates had fallen and divorce rates remained relatively modest. Also births outside marriage had fallen to low levels during the period so that a very high proportion of children grew up together with both their parents.

The trend over recent decades has been to detach parenthood and marriage. This is seen both in the increase in births outside (or before) marriage and the higher divorce rate. In most situations it is women who remain as lone parents and this has led to suggestions that men have given up on fatherhood in some sense. However, I think that such claims misstate the position. Figures for the presence of fathers at birth, show that this is now the expected pattern. Fathers seem much more involved at the beginning of their children's lives despite the lack of provision for paternity leave. The difficulties come later if the relationship between parents ends. This may lead to a severing of the connection of father and child. Parent-children relationships in our society often depend on the mother and father remaining in the same household. When marriages or cohabitations end, children typically remain with the mother (who within marriage or a cohabitation will have usually been the principal caretaker) and, at best, the fathers become an intermittent visitor in their lives. The general picture is of fathers fading from the lives of their children once they have left the mother's household. Several factors seem to encourage such trends. The mother-child relationship is idealised as the most important bond for children in both child care manuals and in psychological research. Non-residential parental relationships still receive relatively little social support or approval. A similar message has been given by legal and welfare arrangements which emphasise the links between children and the parent-figures *within* the same household. The ideologies of the nuclear family and step-parenting tend to emphasise exclusiveness and relational self sufficiency of the 'new' household. It is a striking piece of evidence that remarriage of either a separated mother or father is associated with a reduction in contact between a non residential father and his children (see Richards, 1993). One may find many other examples of policies which emphasise a notion of parenthood as co-residence; for example, many schools regard the adults who happen to live with children as their 'parents', for the purposes of teacher contact, election of parent governors, etc. The Child Support Agency is a welcome move in a new direction (at least in theory, if not, in its practice) as it gives economic priority to children of first relationships,

Fertility rates in Europe have been changing with what some have described as a new demographic transition with the lowest rates in the southern countries and the highest (and rising rates) in the north. One association that has been pointed out with these trends is the provision of public child care and the extent to which it is made easier, for women in particular, to combine child care and paid employment. It has been suggested that such provision encourages rising fertility. Britain is in a middle position in Europe with respect to such trends. Perhaps the most noticeable recent trend has been the postponement of child bearing (along with postponement of marriage) to later ages. Late child bearing, of course, keep fertility rates low.

Patterns of sexual relations

Sexual relations have become more independent of both marriage and cohabitation. While it is obviously true that sexual intercourse has never been confined to marriage, the evidence suggests that today adults typically have more sexual partners than in the recent past (Johnson et al, 1994). Young people are beginning sexual relationships at earlier ages and have more partners before they begin a cohabitation or marriage. While these relationships may have a strong commitment to sexual monogamy, old patterns may be hard to break (Reibstein and Richards, 1992). Like the higher rates of divorce, the wider range of sexual experience that couples bring to marriage may serve to further emphasise the ideal of monogamy. Similar reasons may have led to the trend of making the wedding itself a more important social event as a way of marking a transition from an earlier phase of life in which the expectations and rules for social and sexual relationships may have been rather different.

Given that the changes in the sexual relations of young people have been relatively recent, it is very difficult to predict the extent that their marriages and cohabitations may follow the patterns of earlier generations. What is striking is that there is very little sign of earlier child bearing associated with earlier sexual relationships. Clearly the separation of sexual relationship from child bearing is now more complete than ever before.

In respect to marriage and cohabitation it seems more likely that there will be consequences of the changing patterns of relationships of young adults. Current ideology may require a sharp change between patterns of relationship for young people as they move into marriage and cohabitation. While many have a series of more or less monogamous relationships before they 'settle down', increasing numbers, especially of young men, may not have ideals of exclusiveness (e.g. Moore and Rosenthal, 1993). It seems a reasonable prediction that such patterns, together with the continuing ideology of the companionate marriage (or cohabitation), are likely to maintain high rates of divorce.

Economic policies

Current policies concerning minimum wages, welfare provision, employment, the distribution of housing and the provision of child care do not aid the quality of life for parents and children, especially those who are less well off. Several trends can be discerned which have combined to bring this about. These include an ideology which attempts to separate off the public and the 'private' world of the family in debates and policies concerning the economy and employment. The 'private' world of the family is seen to be beyond the influence of the State and it is where 'parental responsibility' and other individual qualities are held to be all important. In its extreme form these arguments reduce all relationship in the public sphere to economics and to the claim 'there is no such thing as society'. This has been coupled with a situation where overall incomes have risen, but the effects have been selective so that those at the upper end of the scale have benefited most, while those at the bottom end have become poorer. While the costs of child rearing are considerable, tax and benefit systems have increasingly failed to take account of this so that the real cost of child rearing especially to those on lower incomes has increased. Poverty traps, as well as the difficulty in finding adequate child care, have served to keep many out of the labour force, especially lone mothers, and effectively denied them possibilities of improving their economic position, except through cohabitation or marriage. But that route to economic improvement will usually mean that another household with children will move into poverty.

The retreat of the welfare state has been widespread in the industrialised world (though there are partial exceptions, e.g. Sweden), but, very significantly, it is children and their parents that have borne the brunt of the deterioration. Given the abundant evidence that poor economic and material circumstance reduce children's life chances and make satisfactory social relationships more difficult, the longer term outlook for the present generation is bleak.

Conclusions

In this chapter I have described some recent trends in family life, concentrating on matters related to parents and their children. Changes in family life have been particularly rapid in recent decades and, not surprisingly, these changes have provoked widespread concern and anxieties. But these anxieties have not always been focused on the key changes. We have often failed to develop policies to support family life in the face of these changes. Policies and agencies are the subject of other chapters in this book. I have tried to focus attention on the key areas, ideologies of marriage and cohabitation, child bearing, patterns of sexual relations and the economic position of parents and children.

As past history shows, family life can be very robust. It survives and accommodates to war, economic depression and periods of rapid social change, though such changes can cause great hardship especially to those in weak economic positions. These will usually include a considerable number of those caring for children. While forms of domestic life are evolving rapidly, the family is not in terminal decline – whatever such claims might mean. However, current rapid change may be painful for some and there are casualties. Our aims must be to analyse carefully the changes that are occurring, to identify the groups who have become vulnerable and then to devise social and economic policies to meet their situation.

Acknowledgements

I am grateful to Ginny Morrow for her comments on an earlier draft of this chapter.

References

Bradshaw, J. (1993) *Housing Budgets and Living Standards*. York: Joseph Rowntree Foundation.
Cherlin, A. and Fustenberg, F.K. (1988) The European family. Special issue, *Journal of Family Issues*, 9, No. 3.
Elliott, B.J. and Richards, M.P.M. (1991) Sex and Marriage in the 1960s and 1970s. In D. Clark (ed) *Marriage, Social Change and Domestic Life*. London: Routledge.
Ermisch, J. (1993) Families Oeconomica. A survey of economics of the family. *Scottish Journal of Political Economy*, 40, 357–358.
Finch, J. (1989) *Family Obligations and Social Change*. Cambridge: Polity Press.
Finch, J. and Mason, J. (1993) *Negotiating Family Responsibilities*. London: Routledge.
Harris, C.C. (1990) *Kinship*. Milton Keynes: Open University Press.
International Year of the Family, UK. (1994) *Fact sheets*. London: International Year of the Family.

Johnson, A.M., Wadsworth, J., Wellings, K. and Field, J. (1994) *Sexual Attitudes and Lifestyles.* Oxford: Blackwell Scientific Publications.

Kiernan, K. and Estaugh, U. (1993) *Cohabitation, Extra-marital Child Bearing and Social Policy.* London, Family Policy Studies Centre.

Lewis, S. and Cooper, C. (1988) The transition to parenthood in dual earner couples. *Psychological Medicine,* 2, 289–301.

Losh-Hesselbant, S. (1987) Development of gender roles. In M.B. Sussman and S.K. Steinmetz (eds). *Handbook of Marriage and the Family.* New York: Plenum.

Miller, B.C. (1987) Marriage, family and fertility. In M.B. Sussman and S.K. Steinmatz (eds) *Handbook of Marriage and the Family.* New York: Plenum.

Moore, S. and Rosenthal, D. (1993) *Sexuality in Adolescence.* London: Routledge.

Oppenheim, C. (1993) *Poverty: The Facts.* London, Child Poverty Action Group.

Phillips, R. (1988) *Putting Assunder: A History of Divorce in Western Society.* Cambridge: Cambridge University Press.

Reibstein, J. and Richards, M.P.M. (1992) *Sexual Arrangements.* London: Heinemann/Mandarin.

Richards, M.P.M. (1993) Learning from divorce. In C. Clulow. (ed) *Does Marriage Matter?* London: Karnac Books.

Richards, M.P.M. (1994) The interests of children at divorce. Paper given at the International Conference, *Families and Justice,* Brussels, July 1994 and to appear in the Proceedings.

Roll, J. (1992) *Understanding Poverty. A Guide to the Concepts and Measures.* London: Family Policy Studies Centre.

Utting, D. (1995) *Supporting Families, Preventing Breakdown: a Guide to the Debate About Family and Parenthood.* York: Joseph Rowntree Foundation.

Wilkinson, K. (1994) *No Turning Back: Generations and the Genderquake.* London: Demos.

Appendix.

Sources of demographic and quantitative information about the family

In order to avoid overburdening the text I have not provided a reference for each point taken from official statistics but I have referenced research studies.

A series of Fact Sheets produced by the International Year of the Family UK office (Yalding House, 152 Great Portland Street, London W1N 6AJ) provides an excellent summary, with sources of information about family life. The Family Policy Studies Centre publishes a useful *Bulletin* as well as research reports (231 Baker Street, London NW1 6XE). Official statistics released by Government are generally published by the Stationary Office. Of particular interest, is *Social Trends* compiled by the Central Statistical Office. An excellent overview is given in David Utting's report 'Supporting Family, Preventing Breakdown: A Guide to the Debate About Family and Parenthood' for the Joseph Rowntree Foundation (The Homestead, 40 Water End, York, YO3 6LP). The Joseph Rowntree Foundation is the major funder of research on family life in the UK and its

Findings series give brief, clear summaries of the results of projects they support.

The Commission of the European Communities provides information about EU countries. Of particular help is the European Observatory on National Family Policies (T. Nuelant, Dept of Sociologie, E. van Evenstroat ZC, B–3000 Leuven). Though a little dated, the *Journal of Family Issues* published a wide ranging special issue in 1988 (volume 9, no. 3) on the European family edited by Andrew Cherlin and Frank Furstenberg. Ranging further afield, *Family Matters*, a magazine/newsletter produced by the Australian Institute of Family Studies (300 Queen Street, Melbourne, Victoria 3000, Australia) has much of interest to readers in the UK. The publications data base produced by A.I.F.S. is a valuable aid.

Finally, two words of caution: many statements made about 'Europe' in fact refer to the countries of the European Union rather than geographical Europe. The distinction is an important one as both in Scandinavia and some of the Eastern European countries family life is rather different from that within the EU. The second concerns the wide diversity between the regions of the UK. Often figures that may be taken to refer to the UK as a whole, in fact relate to England and Wales. Even when an overall UK statistic is given, difference in the smaller populations of Scotland, Wales and Northern Ireland will be effectively concealed by the larger numbers from England. A researcher's life is not made easier by the separate publication of some figures by the Welsh, Scottish, and Northern Ireland Offices. 'National' London based organisations often only present figures for England.

4

Family Poverty and the Role of Family Support Work

Gil Long

FAMILY poverty is now widespread in the UK. Over the last ten years people of working age and their children have become increasingly at risk of poverty. The aim of this chapter is to present the facts that demonstrate this (with particular reference to Scotland), to describe briefly the impact of poverty on families and their children, and to argue that family support work has a role to play in helping families to find routes out of poverty.

The growth of poverty

There are many in our society today who are living without basic necessities, as evidenced by the now common sight of young people sleeping rough on our streets, the increasing numbers of people who are having to do without fuel or clean water as a result of disconnections, and those many families and individuals whose applications to the Social Fund for essential items, such as bedding, adequate clothing and living expenses in times of crisis, are turned down. This paper relies on the concept of relative poverty which argues that poverty must be defined relative to the prevailing living standards in society, for the debate is not simply about the basics necessary for survival but about social needs too. Inadequate incomes effectively exclude people from participating in ordinary, everyday activities. There is no 'official' poverty line but two frequently quoted measures are used here to describe the growth of poverty in Scotland: those living below the threshold of 50% less than average income and the numbers of people dependent on income support.

Households below average income

In 1979 five million people or 9% of the UK population lived in households with below 50% of average income (after housing costs) but by 1991/92 this had risen to 13.9 million or 25% of the population. This is particularly astounding since it has been shown that between the early 1960s and the mid 1970s the incidence of poverty actually fell as the numbers of people living in households below half of the national average income decreased from five to around three million people (Goodman and Webb, 1994). Analysis of the figures from 1979 to 1991/92 show that pensioners have become less frequently represented within the 50% below average income bracket whilst the incidence of lone parents and couples with children has increased. Consequently, as Figure 1 shows, it is children who have fared worse as poverty has grown. In 1979 10% of the child population of the UK lived in households with below 50% of average income but by 1991/92 this had risen to 32% or nearly one in three of the child population. Estimates suggest that in Scotland the figures are even worse with 38% of the children living at this level (CPRU, 1994).

Figure 1

Growth of poverty in UK 1979-1991/92
% of children and all population below 50% average income (after housing costs)

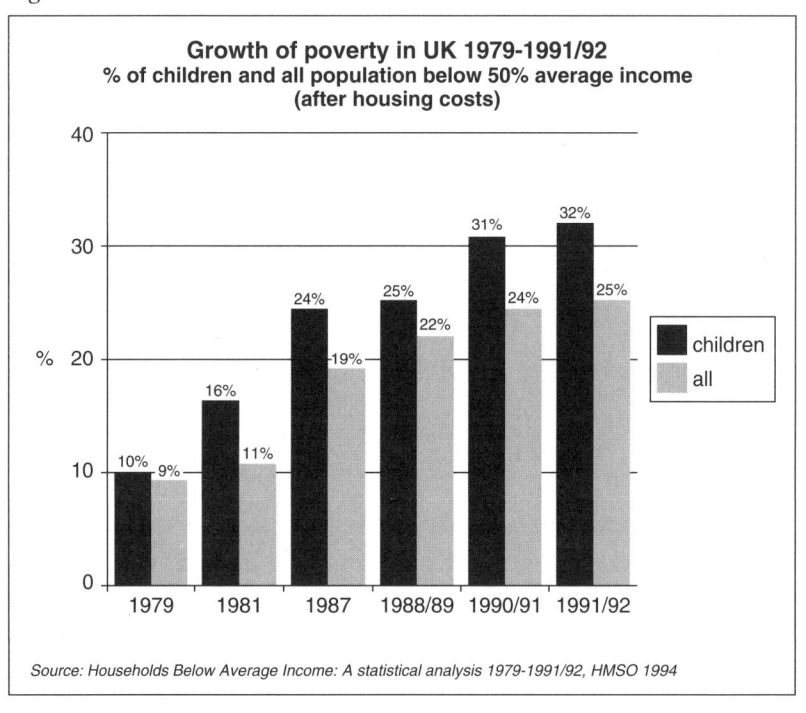

Year	children	all
1979	10%	9%
1981	16%	11%
1987	24%	19%
1988/89	25%	22%
1990/91	31%	24%
1991/92	32%	25%

Source: Households Below Average Income: A statistical analysis 1979-1991/92, HMSO 1994

Figure 2 shows the composition of those living below 50% of average income in 1991/92. Although pensioners and single people make up significant proportions of the population living at this level, the largest proportion are families with children, amounting to over seven million individuals. One factor here is that the risk of poverty may be viewed as varying over the life cycle, with the costs of caring for children and bringing them up making families more vulnerable.

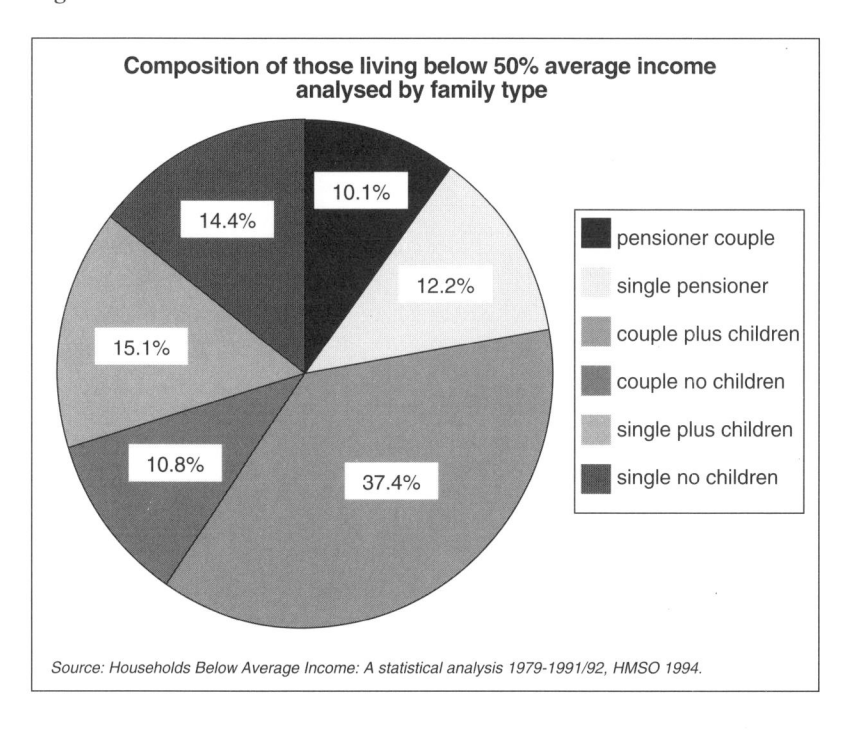

Figure 2

Composition of those living below 50% average income analysed by family type

- pensioner couple: 10.1%
- single pensioner: 12.2%
- couple plus children: 37.4%
- couple no children: 10.8%
- single plus children: 15.1%
- single no children: 14.4%

Source: Households Below Average Income: A statistical analysis 1979-1991/92, HMSO 1994.

Social security and income support figures

Income support is the benefit which replaced supplementary benefit in 1988 and is the minimum level of income or 'safety net' figure set by the Government. Figures from the Social Security Committee's 'Low Income Families 1979–89' show a similar dramatic rise in poverty and the increasing vulnerability of children, with some 11.3 million people in the UK living at or below the income support level in 1989. Comparable data for Scotland are not available but the latest income support figures show that over one in four children under 16 years old in Scotland live in households dependent on income support.

Clearly there are differences between the two measures. The figures using the threshold of 50% below average income include families and individuals on low pay and other means-tested benefits besides income support, for example family credit. In 1993 50% below average income for a family with two children aged under eleven was £148.00 per week after housing costs. The income support allowance for an equivalent family was £108.75, excluding housing costs. It is important to point out that both measures exclude many who are living below the levels indicated. People who do not claim their benefit are not represented in income support figures. Those living in institutions or hostels and those living rough are not included within the figures for Households Below Average Income. Young people aged 16 and 17 are excluded from the general income support figures since they have no automatic entitlement to benefit. The Scottish figures for severe hardship payment claims, a discretionary payment available to 16/17 year olds who can prove severe hardship and vulnerability, show a 350% rise from 1983–1993 and so demonstrate increasing need amongst young people. Many young people who cannot gain a place on a youth training scheme but who are unable to claim benefit will undoubtedly be putting extra strain on already stretched family resources.

In summary, in the last decade and a half, poverty in the UK has risen dramatically. Depending on which measures are used, between 11 and 13 million people are living in poverty. Further analysis shows that it is people of working age and therefore their children who have fared worst in recent years. Families with children are much more likely to be living in poverty than they were 15 years ago. For such families poverty means having to cut back on basics, struggling to make ends meet and the constant worry and stress of trying to bring up children on inadequate incomes, in the knowledge that their children's long term life chances and opportunities are diminished.

The causes of poverty

The causes of this dramatic rise in poverty are structural; they relate to the economy and government policy and are therefore outwith the control of the individual. The main underlying reason lies in the growing numbers of people who can no longer depend on an adequate and secure income through employment. In addition changes in government policy with respect to benefits, social services and taxation have also led to increased poverty.

Changes in employment

Scotland has always experienced high levels of unemployment and recent estimates show that one third of Scotland's 10.3% unemployed people are long term unemployed, i.e. out of work for over one year (Unemployment Unit,1994). National unemployment figures not only grossly underestimate the numbers of unemployed (some estimates are double the official figures) but they also hide many local variations: concentrations of around 25% unemployment in certain inner city areas; rural areas where jobs are extremely scarce and groups of people who are particularly vulnerable to unemployment.

The changing structure of employment is a crucial factor. As manufacturing industries have declined the only growth areas in the economy have been in mostly insecure and low paid forms of employment such as self employment, part-time and seasonal or temporary work. This shift also represents gender changes in the world of work. The traditional industries were mostly male dominated whilst the growth areas are within the service sectors which offer jobs in female dominated areas of work. These trends are outlined in Figures 3 and 4. The significant factor here is that the 'new' jobs are invariably low paid and this is a major cause of poverty. Such trends have made women even more vulnerable to poverty and the implications of this for tackling poverty are outlined below. Estimates from the Scottish Low Pay Unit show that in 1993 43% of adult employees (full- and part-time workers) earned less than the Scottish Low Pay Unit's threshold of £203.07 per week. Low pay is likely to be an increasing issue after the abolition of the Wages Councils which removed minimum wages in a number of service sector industries (Scottish Low Pay Unit, 1994).

Self employment grew by 50% for males between 1981 and 1989 and by 100% for females, but this is no guarantee of an adequate income (Scottish Enterprise, 1992). Self-employed people are over represented within both the very high and very low earnings brackets with 15% of all self employed people falling within the bottom decile of the income distribution in 1991/92 (HBAI 1994). Moreover, self-employed people often find it difficult to claim benefits such as family credit and housing benefit.

Figure 3

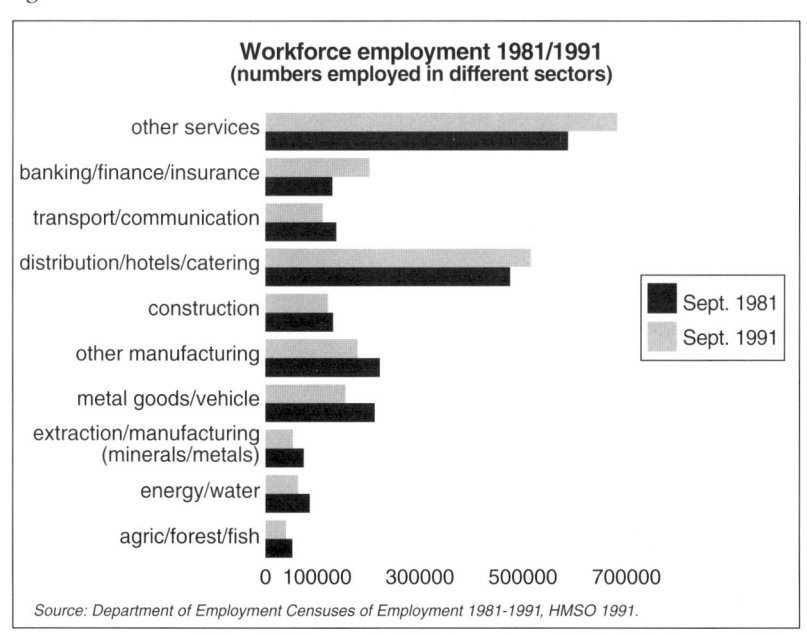

Workforce employment 1981/1991
(numbers employed in different sectors)

Source: Department of Employment Censuses of Employment 1981-1991, HMSO 1991.

Figure 4

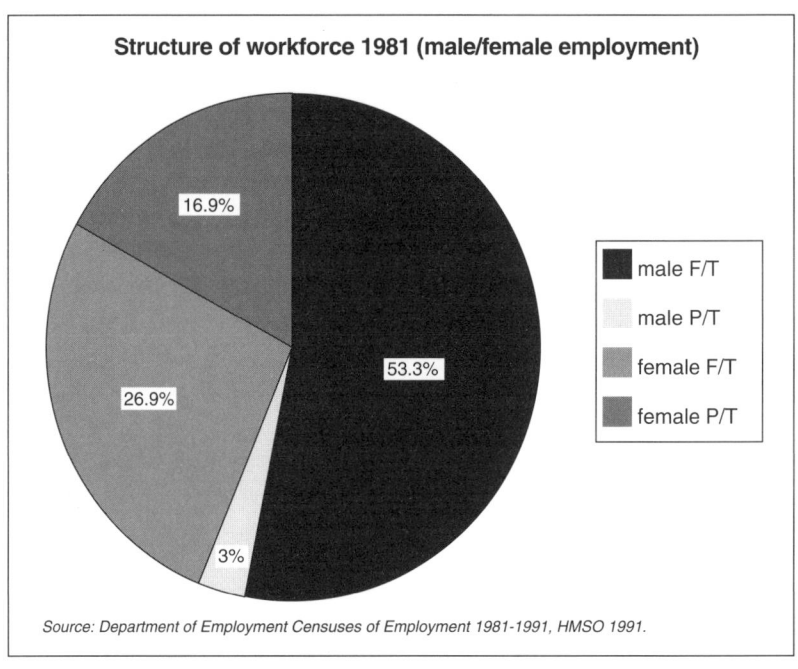

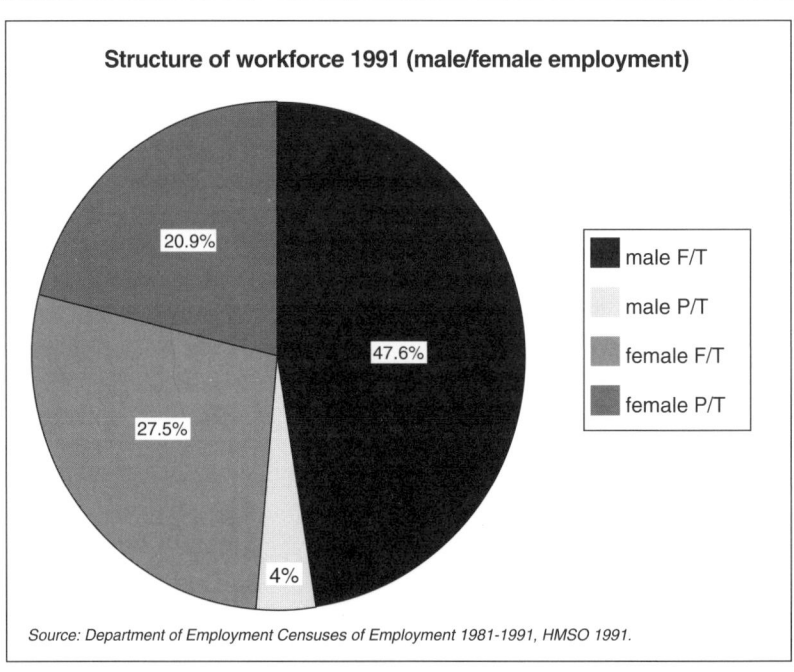

Structure of workforce 1981 (male/female employment)

- male F/T: 53.3%
- male P/T: 3%
- female F/T: 26.9%
- female P/T: 16.9%

Source: Department of Employment Censuses of Employment 1981-1991, HMSO 1991.

Structure of workforce 1991 (male/female employment)

- male F/T: 47.6%
- male P/T: 4%
- female F/T: 27.5%
- female P/T: 20.9%

Source: Department of Employment Censuses of Employment 1981-1991, HMSO 1991.

Changes to benefits and services

Cuts and changes to benefits and services have also contributed to increasing poverty. While the level of benefits rose between 1979 and 1989, the increase was less than half that of the rise in average incomes (Social Security Committee, 1993). A number of changes have affected families in particular. There have been restrictions and cuts in unemployment benefit and other national insurance benefits, with more to come in April 1996. The level of child benefit was frozen from 1988 until 1990 and then only partially uprated. Supplementary single payments for essential items and services were abolished and replaced by the Social Fund, a cash-limited discretionary system which dispenses mostly loans rather than grants.

However, the most pertinent fact is that income support is insufficient to support a family. Calculations for a low cost budget for a family of two adults and two children under eleven on 1993 prices showed that income support was £34 per week short of the required level (Oldfield and Yu, 1993). Families are now more likely to be in poverty because their benefit is simply not enough to cover the costs of caring for their children.

Other changes have affected those claiming in-work benefits such as restriction of the entitlement for free school meals to income support claimants only. In addition cuts in public services have had a direct effect on living standards. For example, local authority housing stock has decreased by 21% since 1982 whilst rents have risen by 195%, five times the increase in average incomes over the same period (CPRU, 1994). Increased charges for services like dental treatment and prescriptions affect the poor disproportionately.

Changes in taxation

Taxation policy over recent years has seen a shift from direct to indirect taxes which weigh more heavily on those on lower incomes. These have included the community charge, in operation from 1989–1993 which was a flat rate for all adults and increases in VAT. These changes, coupled with reductions in the top rates of income tax, have meant that between 1979–1992 the richest 10% of the population have seen an average increase in their incomes of £87 per week whereas the poorest 10% have lost £1 per week (Davis et al in Oppenheim, 1993).

Groups most at risk of poverty

There is clear evidence that we are now living in a society in which income inequalities are growing. Between 1979–1991/92 average incomes rose by 36% but the incomes of the poorest tenth of the population fell by 17%. During the same period the top 10% saw their incomes rise by 62%

(Hansard 1993). The picture is one of an increasing divide between the 'haves' and the 'have nots' – those who have access to adequately paid jobs or incomes and those who do not. Figure 5 shows the percentage of different categories of people falling below 50% of average income and indicates the high risk of poverty for those who are unemployed but also those families which depend on self employment, one wage or on part-time earnings. Even those with full-time work are not guaranteed freedom from poverty.

Figure 5

Percentage of each group with income below 50% of average income (after housing costs)

	1979	1991/92
self employed	15	24
single or couple all in full-time work	1	2
one in full-time work, one in part-time work	1	5
one in full-time work, one not working	4	17
one or more in part-time work	15	32
head or spouse aged 60 or over	20	36
head or spouse unemployed	58	76
other	35	62

Source: Households Below Average Income: A statistical analysis 1979-1991/92, HMSO 1994.

Simplistic analyses frequently seek to explain poverty by placing the blame firmly on the shoulders of the individual. Government spokespersons talk about 'a dependency culture', 'people's unwillingness to work' and 'lack of parental responsibility' but their accusations do not concur with the facts. For example, the chance of being unemployed or in a low paid job is influenced by discrimination in the labour market. People from ethnic minorities are twice as likely to be unemployed as members of the white population and, if they are employed, they are much more likely to work in a low paid job (Amin and Oppenheim, 1992; CPRU, 1994). People with disabilities suffer similar disadvantages in the employment market and also have to provide for the additional costs that disability or long term sickness bring such as special diets, heating, clothing and transport.

Lone parents are particularly vulnerable to poverty because of their difficulties in gaining employment. The incidence of lone parenthood has risen in recent years and in Scotland lone parents now account for about

20% of all family households. 90% of lone parents are women (1991 Census; CPRU, 1994). Research suggests that about 75% of lone parents live on income support and that low levels of predicted pay, lack of employment opportunities and inadequate childcare facilities are the main reasons why lone parents find it hard to work (Glendinning and Millar, 1992). These difficulties stand out against the fact that overall more women are in paid employment than ever before. Whilst the employment of married women increased from 47% to 60% between 1981 and 1990, lone mothers' employment declined over the same period from 45% to 39% (Oppenheim, 1993).

The impact of poverty on families and children

Statistics describe the enormity of the problem of poverty but say little about its effects on families. Poverty damages children's life chances. Children who are brought up in poverty are much more likely to suffer illness; they are also less likely to do well at school. Disadvantage in childhood inevitably has an impact on adult lives. For parents poverty means having to struggle to make ends meet, often with few prospects for improvement and a greater likelihood of getting into debt. In the long term poverty undermines self-respect and lowers the expectations of children and parents alike.

Health

A child from the poorest background is twice as likely to die before reaching the age of 1 than a child from an affluent background. Child admission rates to hospitals for accidents, asthma and gastro-intestinal diseases show similarly steep social gradients (CPRU, 1994). Diet plays an important part in health and there is evidence that children from low income families have poorer diets. As a result their general health is poorer, they are likely to be shorter and to have bad dental health (Cole-Hamilton, 1991). The effects of childhood poverty extend into adulthood bringing lower life expectancy rates. A comparative study of Edinburgh and Glasgow showed that by the age of 25 a general pattern had been established which predisposed Glaswegians to an earlier death from a wide range of diseases. The study concluded that the explanation lay in poverty, poor environments and poor diet (Watt and Ecob, 1992).

The work of Richard Wilkinson and others has shown that income inequality is a crucial factor in explaining health inequalities. He cited studies showing mortality rates in the poorest electoral wards of a northern region of England to be four times higher than in affluent wards. Large variations in the rate of issue of prescriptions were closely associated with differential unemployment rates. Wilkinson commented that:

If risks as great as these resulted from exposure to toxic materials then offices would be closed down and populations evacuated from contaminated areas.

Using international evidence Wilkinson argued that increased inequalities exert a powerful influence on national mortality trends and that improvements in general health of the population depend on tackling the increasing social and economic differentials between rich and poor (Wilkinson, 1994).

Education

Poverty affects a child's chances of success in the educational system. The links between educational achievement and poverty are complex. Not every child who comes from a poor family fails to achieve at school but there is much evidence which shows a strong relationship between low socio-economic class and low achievement. The National Child Development Study demonstrated a very strong correlation between poor literacy skills of parents and low attainment of children. When other factors such as low income were included the correlation was even stronger. The evidence showed that 72% of children from families where the parents had reading problems and who were in the lowest income group were in the lowest reading ability group (ALBSU, 1993). Children who do not perform well at school are less likely to achieve qualifications that will enable them to create better lifestyles for themselves in the future. For those pupils who left school in 1981, for example, only 70% of those with one or two 'O' grades obtained employment compared with over 85% of those with five or more 'O' grades (Raffe in Bondi and Matthews, 1988). Low income, poor housing, unemployment and environmental deprivation combine to disadvantage children. One study of educational attainment in Glasgow showed that a deprived neighbourhood contributes to disadvantage (Garner, 1988). As Figure 6 shows, children from poor homes who live in a deprived area can be doubly disadvantaged.

Explanations of educational disadvantage are complex and research suggests a number of contributing factors. Parents on low incomes have less to spend on books, educational toys, extra curricular activities or outings to museums, plays and concerts, whether organised by the family or the school. People who are unemployed or in low status jobs frequently experience a sense of powerlessness which may mean that they are less able to support their children's education or find their way around the educational system. Recent changes to educational policy which emphasise parental choice and encourage schools to specialise and select pupils will exacerbate disadvantage and inequalities; for poor families the local school is the only real choice.

Figure 6

Probability of attaining 3 or more SCE Highers according to categories of home and area disadvantage	
Disadvantaged home and disadvantaged area	3%
Disadvantaged home and advantaged area	22%
Advantaged home and disadvantaged area	26%
Advantaged home and advantaged area	70%

Source: Educational attainment in Glasgow: The role of neighbourhood deprivation, by Catherine Garner. Centre for Educational Sociology, 1988.

Family budgets

Many studies illustrate the more immediate effects of poverty on the lives of parents and their children. Living on a low income means having to cut back on basics such as food, fuel and clothing. Huby and Dix (1992) document evidence from some 1,700 people who applied to the Social Fund in 1990 in which 87% of respondents reported being really worried because they had not been able to find the money for essential expenses. The main problem facing families with children was providing enough food to eat at each meal and many reported leaving other bills unpaid in order to provide clothing and footwear. Many families were short of basic household items: 27% did not have adequate bedding, 14% did not have adequate floor coverings in the living area, 17% did not have sufficient beds or cots for each member of the family and 30% did not have a washing machine.

A survey of parents on benefit showed that one in five parents and one in ten children had gone hungry in the preceding month because of lack of food and no child was eating a healthy diet (NCH, 1991). Such studies show that living on a low income does not simply mean having to do without luxuries but that families are going short of the basic necessities. Living on a low income inevitably brings material hardship and very restricted lifestyles for parents and children alike.

The rise in poverty has been mirrored by a similar rise in debt as families have borrowed to make ends meet. Studies show that those who are most likely to be in debt are low income families with children but there is very little evidence to suggest that debt is associated with consumerism, rather with the everyday problems of budgeting (Berthoud and Kempson, 1992). In a recent study which looked at the coping mechanisms employed by families living on low incomes the authors reported that only a minority of families managed to retain an equilibrium in their budgets and avoid falling into arrears. Whether families borrowed and juggled their bills in order to get by or deprived themselves both materially and socially as they made the bills a priority, they all suffered ill health and high levels of stress (Kempson, 1994).

That there should be so much evidence of educational disadvantage, health inequalities, material hardship, debt and despair is an indictment of current policies and a waste of financial and human resources on a scale which this country can ill afford. However, the argument still has to be won that poverty is not the fault of the individual and that it is within the power of government to address the underlying causes of poverty: unemployment, low wages, inadequate benefits and unfair taxation.

Family policy and family support work

Macro problems require macro solutions and these are properly the responsibility of central government. But there is also a role for organisations that work with families and their work should not be seen as simply ameliorative, a patching up activity which only tackles the symptoms. Successful community-led initiatives provide models for effective family policies and offer immediate and practical help. Local organisations have a vital role to play in campaigning on poverty issues and working in ways which help those who are suffering the injustice of poverty to speak out in their own defence. This is illustrated by the work of Save the Children.

Family support is a general title but in the context of Save the Children's work usually means community based family centres which offer a variety of services: day care facilities for children ranging from crèches to nursery classes; out of school activities; adult education and training for parents; drop-in facilities; community health groups; welfare rights, money advice and credit union facilities; safety equipment exchange schemes and so on. Save the Children's family centres are not be viewed within the 'crisis oriented' model of interventions which offer 'therapeutic' help to families and children in need, but are firmly based within the community development framework. They provide practical responses to locally defined need. The principles of open access, self referral and user participation are fundamental to this approach. The anti-poverty strategy which underpins this work has two themes. The services seek to provide 'better beginnings' for children and 'new opportunities' for adults.

Save the Children's Rosemount project based in Royston in North East Glasgow illustrates this approach. Census data for the Royston area reveal the extent of deprivation. The unemployment level is 44%. Lone parent families account for 43% of all households with children. 69% of children of school age receive free school meals indicating that their family is dependent on income support and 76% receive school clothing grants available to families claiming income support or family credit. These figures compare with regional averages for Strathclyde of 30% and 41% respectively (1991 census data). Much of the housing is of poor quality comprising old style tenements and multi-storey flats with all the associated disadvantages for families with young children. Dampness and fuel poverty are problems which many Royston families face every day. It is a hostile environment in which to bring up children where there are few safe play areas, poor community facilities, a lack of services and few prospects for finding a way out of poverty. Urban regeneration projects are beginning to have an impact on the area and it is clear that where physical improvements in appearance and facilities have been made they have a generally uplifting effect.

The Rosemount Project provides community childcare for the area of Royston alongside training courses which offer vocational qualifications for women in information technology and childcare. In common with many of Save the Children's projects, Rosemount focuses on work with women. There are good reasons for this.

Women are particularly vulnerable to poverty. Lone parenthood is one explanation of this. A further reason is that employment available to women is frequently temporary, part-time and low paid. Their role as primary carers of children and inadequate childcare facilities condemn many women to the least well paid and insecure sectors of the labour market. The only jobs which fit with domestic responsibilities are those which offer few prospects of an adequate living wage.

Female employment has been the only real growth area in the UK in the last few years rising by 20% since the early 1970s whilst male employment has fallen by the same percentage. Full-time work, predominantly a male preserve, has contracted by 15% whilst part-time work, which is 80% female, has risen by 77%. Lone mothers are much less likely to work than women living within partnerships. However, women with an employed partner are much more likely to be in work themselves. The most significant rise in female employment has been amongst women with higher qualifications (Balls and Gregg, 1994).

These trends suggest that female earnings are central to family income and will continue to be so for the foreseeable future. Any intervention which seeks to combat poverty must therefore enable women to compete for the skilled and better paid jobs and to help those who find it most difficult to work, namely lone parents.

It is important that these arguments are not seen as furthering a low wage economy. Measures to promote women's employment have to take place alongside continued pressure to raise women's wages and for reform of the benefits system which discourages women whose partners are unemployed from taking jobs.

There is a further reason for promoting women's economic independence through employment since there is much evidence to show that when additional income is in the hands of women a larger proportion of household budgets is devoted to food, health and education. Children are therefore the direct beneficiaries (Pahl, in Oppenheim,1993). International studies support this conclusion showing, for example, that in Brazil children's weight is eight times greater if the extra income is in the hands of the mother (Thomas in Balls and Gregg, 1994).

Rosemount's approach is to pursue the anti-poverty strategy by opening up new opportunities for women through gaining vocational qualifications and to offer high quality childcare for their children. Within Rosemount childcare is provided for all ages of pre-school children from babies through to children whose next step is the primary school. Childcare should not be seen simply as the vehicle which enables parents to train or work, although this function is obviously crucial. There is now mounting evidence to show that good childcare in early years enhances educational equality of opportunity and helps to form young people who are better able to cope in today's world. In Rosemount the emphasis is on quality childcare which will enhance children's long term life chances. The childcare curriculum embraces children's physical and intellectual developmental needs but also includes important social aspects, for example, the anti-racist dimension. Childcare staff spend time working with parents to ensure their children's progress. For each child a diary is kept which details his or her development and contains examples of the child's work. These diaries are the property of the child and his or her parents, underlining the principle that childcare is not seen as a substitute for parenting but an additional element in which parent and childcare staff participate.

For many women the barriers to undertaking training or further education are formidable. The availability of adequate, accessible and affordable childcare facilities is one factor but the lack of confidence which many women experience is an equally daunting hurdle that has to be overcome. Many of the trainees at Rosemount left school with few qualifications, may not have held jobs before having children and are therefore understandably frightened by the prospect of putting themselves forward for training courses. Staying at home to look after children is itself an isolating activity and as a result many mothers have very low self esteem.

The type of courses organised by Rosemount and the counselling and ongoing support provided by the training staff provide the encouragement which enables the women to achieve high success rates in gaining qualifications. Most unusually for a community project, Rosemount has become an accredited Scotvec training centre enabling it to award its students nationally recognised vocational qualifications. In 1993 only six of the 63 trainees who joined the courses had any prior qualifications, yet 45 gained middle level Scotvec certificates and a further 18 gained qualifications at the basic level. Of the 103 trainees who studied at Rosemount during 1992 and 1993, 23% gained employment and another 37% went on to further education. Whilst this is clearly not a 100% success rate these figures have to be viewed within the overall economic position of the area. It is also important to note that these figures reflect the position of the women within three months of the course ending. Rosemount's courses are financed by the European Social Fund (ESF) and following ESF criteria courses end in December. Most further and higher education courses do not begin until the following August or October, hence there is a considerable gap before the students can 'move on'. There are also positive outcomes from the training that go unrecorded, such as the number of women who subsequently become involved in community activities.

Many women who do find jobs or other training or education courses to attend find that the lack of childcare poses real problems. Although Rosemount is able to help some of its past trainees, demand outstrips supply and currently there are 101 parents awaiting childcare places. Without adequate and affordable childcare women simply cannot 'move on'. In addition the benefit system operates to trap many women in poverty since the employment available and wages on offer are inadequate to compensate for the loss of benefits and the additional costs of working such as childcare and travel.

There are other aspects to the Rosemount project which the community development approach supports. The childcare facility itself provides employment for some of the former trainees who have gained qualifications in childcare and there are now more jobs on offer as the project expands its after school provision. A further development has been the introduction of a welfare rights and money advice clinic, which initially served the project but is now training project users as advisers with the aim of offering a service to the wider community.

Participation is a key principle. A project users committee has a role in directing the project and helps to organise activities which include fundraising to provide subsidised holidays for families, first aid and self defence courses, health promotion activities and support groups of various kinds.

Thus at Rosemount family support means more than simply access to childcare and training. It means being involved in an active community with others who find themselves in a similar situation. It offers an end to isolation and the exclusion that poverty brings, a chance to discard feelings of guilt or failure and to regain the confidence that is needed to retrain and to compete in the world of work. Too often being poor also means having poor access to all kinds of services, to health care, to housing, or education services. Those families that manage to maintain or rebuild their self esteem are better equipped to fight off the stigma of poverty and demand their equal rights.

Conclusions

The problems and messages illustrated here by the Rosemount project are echoed in many parts of the country and are being addressed by similar locally led initiatives. Tackling the scale of poverty in the UK today requires radical social and economic change but also effective policies which provide the support and services necessary to enable families to care for their children. Such measures are urgently required to ensure every child's right under the United Nations Convention to an adequate standard of living, to education on the basis of equality of opportunity and to the highest attainable standard of health.

References

ALBSU (1993) *Parents and their Children: The Intergenerational Effects of Poor Basic Skills.*

Amin, K. and Oppenheim, C. (1992) *Poverty in Black and White: Deprivation and Ethnic Minorities.* London: Child Poverty Action Group.

Balls, E. and Gregg, P. (1994) *Work and Welfare: Tackling the Jobs Deficit.* London: Institute for Public Policy Research.

Berthoud, R. and Kempson, E. (1992) *Credit and Debt: The PSI Report.* London: Policy Studies Institute.

Bondi, L. and Matthews, M.H. (1988) *Education and Society.* London: Routledge.

Cole-Hamilton, I. (1991) *Poverty Can Seriously Damage Your Health.* London: Child Poverty Action Group.

Department of Social Security (1994) *Households Below Average Income: A Statistical Analysis 1979-1991/92.* London: HMSO.

Garner, C. (1988) *Educational Attainment in Glasgow: The Role of Neighbourhood Deprivation.* Edinburgh: Centre for Educational Sociology.

Glendinning, C. and Millar, J. (1992) *Women and Poverty in Britain.* Hemel Hempstead: Harvester Wheatsheaf.

Goodman, A. and Webb, S. (1994) *For Richer, For Poorer: The Changing Distribution of Income in the United Kingdom 1961–1991.* London: Institute of Fiscal Studies.

Hansard, 27 July 1993, col 1010.

Huby, M. and Dix, G. (1992) *Evaluating the Social Fund.* DSS Research Report No 9. London: HMSO.

Kempson, E. (1994) Strategies Used By Low Income Families With Children to Make Ends Meet, *Findings 53.* York: Joseph Rowntree Foundation.

Long, G. (1994) *Poverty Briefing Pack. Glasgow:* Child Poverty Resource Unit, Save the Children.
NCH *Food and Nutrition Survey* (1991).
Oldfield, N. and Yu, A.C.S. (1993) *The Cost of a Child.* London: Child Poverty Action Group.
Oppenheim, C. (1993) *Poverty: The Facts.* London: Child Poverty Action Group.
Scottish Enterprise (1992) *Women's Access to Jobs and Skills in Scotland.*
Scottish Low Pay Unit (1994) Low pay in Scotland in 1993, in *Payline* No. 16.
Social Security Committee Second Report (1993) *Low Income Statistics: Low Income Families (LIF) 1979–1989.* London: HMSO.
Unemployment Unit and Youthaid (1994) in *Working Brief* No. 57.
Watt, G. and Ecob, R. (1992) Mortality in Glasgow and Edinburgh: A Paradigm of Inequality in Health. *Journal of Epidemiology and Community Health* No 46.
Wilkinson, R. (1994) Divided We Fall. *British Medical Journal* April 30.

5

FAMILIES AND THE LAW: POLICING OR SUPPORT?

Kathleen Marshall

Introduction

NINETEEN-ninety-four was the International Year of the Family. It was also a year in which we were beginning to see the fruits of an earlier International Year sponsored by the United Nations – the 1979 International Year of the Child. This led directly to the drafting of a Convention on the Rights of the Child, which was passed by the UN in 1989 and ratified by the UK in 1991. The UK government's first report to the UN on the measures it has taken to implement the Convention was submitted in March 1994.

By no stretch of the imagination could the Convention on the Rights of the Child be seen as an individualistic, anti-family document. The Preamble proclaims that:

> '...the family, as the fundamental group of society and the natural environment for the growth and well-being of all its members and particularly children, should be afforded the necessary protection and assistance so that it can fully assume its responsibilities within the community.'

It would, however, be foolish to deny the existence of some tensions in balancing respect for the family as a unit and an institution, with the rights of the child as set out in the Convention. These consist of children's rights to:
- participation in decisions which affect them
- protection from abuse and neglect
- provision of services to promote survival and development.

If children are to be recognised as having rights as individuals, there must be some mechanism for monitoring implementation of those rights, and for intervening when they are not respected.

There is nothing radically new in this observation. The development of family law, in principle and in application, has been towards greater recognition of the individual rights of family members to be protected by the state against the excesses of the family's more powerful members. Insofar as law and policy seek to uphold the institution of the family, they seek to respect as far as possible the privacy and autonomy of the family. As they seek to protect the interests of the weaker individual members of families, including children, they must sanction some sort of policing role. There must be a means of identifying those family members at risk, and the power to intervene to provide protective measures. There is an inbuilt tension between the aim of the law to support families and the necessity of 'policing' them, in a broad sense, in the interest of individual members.

This chapter aims to explore the inter-relationship of the 'policing' and supportive functions of the law in relation to families, and the allocation of roles in pursuit of these aims. Is it legitimate to keep these functions together? Can they be divided? Who should be charged with carrying them out? This analysis will be made with particular reference to Scotland.

Policing and support

The Collins English Dictionary defines the verb 'police' as 'to regulate, control or keep in order by means of a police or similar force,' or 'to observe or record the activity or enforcement' of something. The 'policing' function can therefore be regarded as wider than the recognised functions of the police.

The aims of family support services were described by Gibbons (1990), as being,

'to relieve stress and promote the welfare of children...But, different aims may also be distinguished at different, though overlapping points along a continuum.'

The dual role of the current law in policing and supporting families is manifest in the provisions of the Social Work (Scotland) Act 1968. Part 2 of the Act addresses the 'Promotion of social welfare by local authorities.' Section 12 obliges local authorities to make appropriate provision for the promotion of social welfare. In particular, the local authority is empowered to provide assistance to diminish the need for a child under 18 to be received into care, or referred to a children's hearing, which might result in a compulsory placement in care or under supervision. Compulsory measures of care are the concern of Part 3 of the Act, which provides for intervention of varying degrees in the interests of the child. Part 2 is therefore largely concerned with support, and Part 3 with 'policing' in the broad sense of that word.

A question sometimes arises about the point at which family support ends and a need for compulsory care begins. There are two aspects to this:

- the general issue of balancing the rights of the individual with the autonomy and privacy of the family unit – a legal structures issue
- the particular issue of recognition of the transition from the supportive to the protective in the experience of a particular family – a professional practice issue.

Legal structures in Scotland

The Scottish legal system currently operates on the presumption that the interests of parents and children coincide, and that parents are normally the best people to represent those interests.

Private law

In private law matters (such as divorce, separation, custody and access) there is no undue interference by the state. In some areas, mediation services exist, some of which now have services to support children affected by parental separation. The general strategy is, however, to support parents in reaching a decision about their children. If they fail to do so, the court will impose a solution.

The court is obliged, by Section 8 of the Matrimonial Proceedings (Scotland) Act 1958, to satisfy itself about the welfare of any children involved before granting a divorce. Sutherland (1991) suggests that these matters often proceed on the basis of sworn statements by the adults involved. The voice of the children concerned, if it is heard at all, is heard through the parents, with no check upon its accuracy.

In some cases the court may appoint a matrimonial reporter or curator ad litem to investigate and report on matters related to the child's welfare, but there is no clear expectation of how they should fulfil their role, the extent to which they should consult children nor indeed the expertise required to communicate effectively with children.

Many parents would resist further involvement by the legal system. There is a fear that children may be involved inappropriately and be given unhelpful responsibility for the making of painful decisions. There is also probably a reluctance to allow the state to intervene and 'police' the family, unless there is positive proof that this is necessary. At the same time, it is the experience of the author that children who have been in these situations often complain that they felt excluded and would have welcomed greater involvement. A recent consultation with young people showed that many were adamant that children's views on these matters should be ascertained and taken seriously (Scottish Office, 1994). The question arises – how can our legal structures identify those children whose views and interests indicate a need for their legal and professional support, without undue intrusion and policing of the family?

Public law

In the public law arena, the same presumption operates in dealing with the promotion of social welfare under the 1968 Act and the protection of children. Even in cases where there is a referral to the children's hearing on the ground that the child is possibly in need of compulsory measures of care, Lockyer (1994) asserts that:

> *The family is the principal focus of treatment and remedy...A major theme of the Kilbrandon Report was partnership with parents and children in seeking to resolve problems.* (p.119.)

The Kilbrandon Report (1964) was the work of a government appointed committee which had been set up:

> *To consider the provisions of the law of Scotland relating to the treatment of delinquents and juveniles in need of care or protection or beyond parental control and, in particular, the constitution, powers and procedure of the courts dealing with such juveniles.*

The committee's proposals were largely enacted in the Social Work (Scotland) Act 1968 which introduced a system of children's hearings to deal with the cases of children who had committed offences or who were for other reasons in need of care, defined in Section 32(3) of the Act as 'protection, control, guidance and treatment'. The philosophy underlying the new system was that offending behaviour by children was indicative of a need for care rather than punishment. The commission of an offence by a child was therefore only one of a number of grounds of referral to a children's hearing.

A children's hearing is a largely informal forum comprising three trained members of the public drawn from a 'children's panel'. A new office of Reporter to the children's panel was created. Although currently employed by the local authority, the Reporter has an independent status and great discretion in making decisions about whether children should be referred to a hearing.

Children's hearings do not adjudicate on disputed matters of fact or law. They can consider a case only when the grounds of referral have either been accepted by the child concerned and his or her parents, or proved in proceedings in the Sheriff Court. Where these conditions are fulfilled, the hearing discusses with the family and relevant professionals what action should be taken in the interest of the child. Disposals available to the hearing are in the form of supervision requirements which can involve the child living at home, with other family members, or in a foster home, residential school or children's home.

Since the introduction of the hearings system in 1971, there has been a significant change in the pattern of referrals, reflecting an increased awareness of the need to protect children, often from their own parents. Lockyer (1994) says:

> *In the first decade after the system's introduction in 1971 the large majority of hearings dealt with children who had committed offences and truants... Now the majority of hearings and supervision requirements relate to cases where the grounds of referral are concerned with child neglect or abuse.* (p.122.)

This has resulted in an increase in the number of cases in which the grounds are not accepted by the parents and the case goes to proof in the Sheriff court. Lockyer also acknowledges that:

> *There is now a greater diversion from hearings and more voluntary support offered to families.* (p.124.)

The implication of this would seem to be that those cases which do end up before a hearing are the difficult ones in which attempts at voluntary support are either regarded as inappropriate, or have been tried and failed – and it is still thought that the children may be in need of compulsory measures of care.

Who represents the children's interests in these situations? The panel members would argue that they do and that is indeed the case when the final decision is made. But they are limited to consideration of the information which is put before them and to what they can glean from discussions at the hearing. Some children may be able to speak up at a hearing, whatever the circumstances, some may only be able to speak up when the parents are out of earshot, and some may not feel able to speak up at all. The Scottish Office (1994) quotes one young respondent:

> *I was stuck in the middle of my Mum and Dad as if we were a cosy wee family. Nobody seemed to see the pressure my Mum and Dad were putting on me just by a movement or a look.* (p.4.)

Social workers might argue that they represent the children's interests, yet there is increasing evidence, referred to by Lockyer, that:

> *In some areas there has been growing departmental control exercised over social workers attending hearings.* (p.125.)

Kearney (1992) also noted this tendency and recommended that it be reversed.

Reporters may see themselves as promoters of the child's interests, and indeed, they too perform this function, but, as Duquette (1994) argues, whilst the role of the Reporter is valuable and unique:

> *The child advocate role...requires independence and is, therefore, incompatible with the other duties of the Reporter.* (p.139.)

Safeguarders

Following on from some tragic child abuse cases in England in which it was clear that the interests of the parent and child diverged, the chairman of a children's hearing, or the sheriff in a disputed case, was given a power to appoint a person to safeguard the interests of the child in the proceedings, if it was considered that there was or might exist a conflict of interest between the child and the parent. In practice, Safeguarders (as they have come to be called) have been very little used since their introduction in 1985. The system operates on the presumption that parents are still the best people to represent their children's interest. Given the change in pattern of referrals, the question arises whether that presumption should now change. This could mean that a Safeguarder or child advocate should be appointed in every case coming before a children's hearing. A variation of that proposal would be that such an appointment would be made unless it had been specifically shown to be unnecessary.

Lockyer (1994) argues against universal appointment of such persons, whilst Duquette (1994) argues in favour. Lockyer's argument is that:

> 'The presumption of a need for separate advocacy presupposes a divided family, where neither parent (nor social worker, nor substitute carer) can adequately support a child in and beyond a hearing... In general, the best advocate for a child is firstly a parent and secondly a social worker.' (p.141.)

Duquette responds by pointing out some difficulties in a selective approach to advocacy:

> Who will decide who needs an advocate and on what basis will that decision be made? Should the parents decide? They may have a conflict of interest and may not be truly objective. Should the Reporter decide? Deciding whether to appoint an advocate may require looking into the details of the matter and maybe even pre-judging the case... What criteria for appointment of a child advocate on a selective basis would guarantee that children are provided assistance on an equal basis? The UN Convention speaks to 'every child deprived of his or her liberty' having access to legal and other appropriate assistance. (p.143.)

The crux of the matter is that the hearing system was set up primarily to engage with young delinquents and their families on the basis of partnership. Is that approach adequate or honest in dealing with child protection cases? It is submitted that it is now time for the presumption to be reversed. In cases where diversionary measures have failed or are considered inappropriate, it should be presumed that a conflict of interests exists, unless the contrary is demonstrated. Compulsory care proceedings are not just about support; they are about 'policing' in the broad sense of that word. Justice, for families and children, requires that this be openly acknowledged in our legal structures.

Professional practice

Similar issues can arise in particular cases operating outwith the compulsory care system. These also raise questions about policing or support.

Although the general provision of social welfare services is supposed to apply to all, the focus in legislation on 'prevention of reception into care', combined with the ever present scarcity of resources, means that the provision is more likely to be used for assistance in cases where there already exists some basis for concern (See Gibbons, Chapter 6). 'Observing or recording' (elements of the Collins Dictionary definition of the verb 'police' referred to above) are almost inevitably involved, if only on an informal basis. If concerns persist or grow, there is the possibility of intervention. It is probably safe to assume that users of services are aware of the powers of intervention which the social work authorities have, if not in detail, at least in some generalised and possibly even exaggerated way. They may then be reluctant to become involved with the authorities and use the resources provided by them, for fear of support escalating into intervention. Doubt is also cast on the honesty of the supportive relationship, where one partner has the potential to draw on an authority and reservoir of legal provisions which can radically alter the balance of the relationship.

Two questions arise from this:
- Is it legitimate to keep the policing and support functions linked, given that there can be tensions in balancing support for the family as a unit with protection of the child and promotion of the child's welfare?
- Is it possible to divide the functions?

Is it legitimate to keep the functions together?

Gibbons et al. (1990) referred to the view that the development of preventive services represented:

> *A form of tutelage, in which sanitary and educative objectives were joined with methods of economic and moral surveillance.* (p.9.)

Reference is also made to criticism of the English equivalent of Section 12 at that time on the basis that it represented a threat to civil liberties. These provisions:

> *Enabled coercive state power to be extended over a much wider group of families... Poor families were forced to turn to social workers for material aid in crisis; but because there was not enough for everyone some rationing device*

> *had to be used, and that was compliance. To get material help families had to submit to the casework plan and accept (the) department's control.* (p.16.)

The same kind of dynamic can also exist where compliance is obtained, not through the carrot of material aid, but through the potential stick of more formal intervention. Families may 'go along' with 'voluntary' involvement of social workers, because the stigma and concerns about compulsory measures are even more worrying. So there may be a 'protection' agenda operating through 'supportive' measures. It could be argued that this is quite in accord with the philosophy of partnership with parents that has gained an increasingly high profile in recent years, but the blurring of the boundaries does raise some concerns, both for the families involved and for the workers. Families may find themselves wandering down the route of compliance and intervention, unsure of the point at which they ought to take advice to protect their legal position, and afraid of the consequences if they do. 'Will this be seen as an admission of guilt?' is, in the author's experience, a common question posed by parents in this situation. Also, professional workers have to operate within an ambivalent role, of friend/supporter and potential assessor and authority figure.

Is it therefore possible to dispel the ambivalence, for families and workers, by dividing the roles and allocating them to different people?

Can the functions be divided?

An attempt to distinguish the functions was made by Lord Clyde in *The Report of the Inquiry into the Removal of Children from Orkney in February 1991* (Clyde 1992):

> *One problem for social workers is the reconciliation in the public's perception of their investigative role and their caring role. The investigatory duty should always be seen as complementary to their caring and supportive role and should never be given a primacy of position. While Section 37 (1A)(a) requires the making of enquiries, that is only the case where a local authority has received information that a child may be in need of compulsory measures of care and further enquiry is necessary. Social Workers should not be and should not be seen to be spies or detectives but should be recognised as agents for the provision of advice, guidance and assistance.* (para.19.26.)

This emphasis on the supportive role of social work is complemented by a strong emphasis on the investigative role of the police:

> *In the working out of the joint approach there must be a clear understanding of the tasks to be carried out by each agency. At the early stage of any possible action the pursuit and recovery of evidence is a matter for the police. The social work profession is not authorised, designed or trained to do this. The*

> *Social Work Department are bound to make enquiries under Section 37(1A) of the Act of 1968 but that only arises where they have received information that a child may be in need of compulsory measures of care and they have no obligation to make enquiries if they are satisfied that such enquiries are unnecessary. They may thus ascertain whether or not there is a case to be investigated but the investigation should be undertaken by the police.* (para.15.31.)

This investigative role is distinguished from what might be regarded as a wider 'policing' role related to the discovery of child abuse:

> *The discovery of sexual abuse should not be seen as the preserve or monopoly of any agency. On the contrary every agency which has any involvement with children should be watchful for any signs which may reflect the existence of abusive conduct.* (para.15.34.)

It is recognised that schools have a particularly important role to play in the identification of child abuse. Great emphasis is placed on the need to maintain as much confidentiality as possible so as not to affect adversely the relationship between the teacher and the family. Schools are also enjoined to develop close relationships with the social work department, to whom their concerns will presumably be forwarded. This recognition of the possible adverse effect on relationships with families consequent upon the teachers' known involvement in initiating intervention, does not appear to be applied equally to social workers, who are charged with being the main instrument of intervention, whilst at the same time not being 'spies or detectives' but providers of advice and assistance.

Although distinctions may be made between the broad 'policing' role of social work and the investigatory role of the police, the perceived power of social workers means that, in terms of the perceived impact of their intervention, there may be little difference between them and the police. To many, the stigma and deprivation of having one's children removed at the conclusion of child protection proceedings may seem every bit as draconian as the stigma and deprivation of loss of individual liberty through imprisonment at the end of a criminal process. The implication for social workers is a confusion of roles, and a mismatch between their official persona as helpers and supporters and the public perception of them as powerful pseudo-police.

Some of this perception may be played down as a misconception by a public which overrates the power of social workers and underestimates the extent to which their actions must be sanctioned by external authorities (the courts, the children's hearing), but it must also be acknowledged that the *de facto* power of social workers is quite considerable. Child care law is not just about adjudicating on disputed matters of fact; it is about reaching decisions which will best serve the interests of children. Lawyers, sheriffs and judges are not trained to make this kind of assessment and must therefore rely heavily on others, such as social workers, who are deemed fit to do so. This was acknowledged in the Clyde Report:

> *Anyone applying for an Order for the removal of a child must carefully assess the evidence on which they are seeking it since it is essentially on their initiative that the Order is being obtained. In a situation of urgency there may be little or no opportunity to seek advice. Nor can the burden be passed on to the Sheriff or JP who necessarily has to rely on a statement by the applicant, is not there to serve as an adviser and while able to form an objective view is less well placed to explore the situation or to ascertain the facts than is the applicant... The judicial authority is...of symbolic rather than practical value. Of course there may well be occasions when the Sheriff or JP may not be persuaded by the presentation that an order should be granted. But the extent to which such a check is available depends critically and significantly on the completeness of the presentation which is made by the applicant. Essentially the practical decision that the child ought to be removed is one on which the applicant must be wholly satisfied.* (para.16.12.)

In a sense, we are all expected to be 'spies' so far as child protection is concerned. We are not all obliged, or even encouraged, to be 'detectives.' On the contrary, we are encouraged to pass the information on to social workers, who then fall under the investigative duty referred to by Lord Clyde; the duty under s.37(1A) of the 1968 Act to make enquiries, and refer to the Reporter if it appears that the child may be in need of compulsory measures of care. In other words – to be detectives.

Lord Clyde argued that 'The investigatory role should always be seen as complementary to their caring role.' Is that an ideal that can be achieved? Social workers do have *de facto* power. They can, and in many cases must, do something with the information which they receive or come across. Their role is inherently ambiguous and evokes an ambivalent response from their clients.

It is submitted that, insofar as social workers have legal powers and legal duties to investigate and initiate intervention in the lives of families, it is not possible to separate out their policing and supportive roles, nor should we expect social work clients to respond on the basis of that distinction.

How are these issues currently being addressed in Scotland?
The UN Convention on the Rights of the Child has had a high profile in the many recent proposals for reform of Scottish child law.

In the private law sphere, the Scottish Law Commission in its 1992 Report on Family Law recommended that parents and others with parental responsibility be placed under an obligation to consult children about major decisions affecting them, and to give due consideration to the child's views, having regard to the child's age and maturity. Where a dispute concerning a child has found its way to court, Rules of Court should ensure that children capable of forming and expressing wishes should be able to have them put directly to the court. The court would be obliged to take account of any children's views so brought before it.

The Commission conceded that the child was 'the central figure in these matters', and that the fact that the parents were in agreement about what should happen did not mean it was any less important to have regard to the child's views. They did however oppose the suggestion that legal representation for a child should be mandatory, not because it was not a good idea, but because it would cost too much:

We do not think that it would be realistic to propose a solution in which separate legal representation had to be arranged for a child in every case where a court was considering an application relating to parental responsibilities and rights. However attractive such an idea may be in theory it would certainly be ruled out on grounds of cost to the legal aid fund. There would be similar objections to any solution which made a report on the child's views mandatory in every case. (para.5.26.)

Public law proposals were contained in the 1993 White Paper 'Scotland's Children – Proposals for Child Care Policy and Law.' These proposals purport to 'incorporate the philosophy of the United Nations Convention on the Rights of the Child.'

The general welfare duty under Section 12 of the 1968 Act is to be widened, to remove the negative connotations of 'prevention of reception into care,' and to 'reflect the positive promotion of children's welfare.' There are indications of a more widespread use of 'respite care,' a service commonly associated with families with children with special needs.

With regard to child protection issues and compulsory measures of care, the proposals seek to balance 'the child's right to protection from harm, where necessary by removal from its source,' and 'the parents' responsibilities for the child and the rights necessary for the exercise of those responsibilities.' This is to be implemented through the introduction of greater legal control over the processes of removing a child from home under a place of safety or 'child protection order,' together with a tightening up of the criteria for authorising such a removal.

Whilst still adhering to the principle that 'parents are responsible for the care of the child,' the proposals go some way towards increased recognition of the possibility that the interests of the parent and child may diverge. Thus, it is proposed to introduce 'a power for hearings to exclude parents from part or parts of hearings in order to hear the views of the child.'

The Paper acknowledges the fact that Safeguarders have been little used, but asserts that the government sees them:

> *As providing a valuable protection for the interests of the child, especially where there are or may be competing pressures within the family. The Government have decided to emphasise the current power of hearings and sheriffs as soon as cases come before them, to consider appointment of Safeguarders in order to ensure that they play an active part in the proceedings. (para.6.18–19.)*

In addition,

> *The Secretary of State has...set in hand a review of the existing role and functions of Safeguarders. The aim is to identify prospects for the extension of their powers and use and to consider how the current arrangements for appointing, training and managing panels of Safeguarders can be improved.* (para.6.20.)

Are these proposals adequate to address the issues identified?

Do these proposals clarify legal and professional structures in order to achieve a better balance between the rights of the individual and the autonomy and privacy of family life? Do they promote good practice in the direction of clarifying and acknowledging the point of transition from the supportive to the protective in the experience of particular families? Do they promote a better inter-relationship of the policing and supportive functions of the law in relation to families?

Insofar as legal structures are concerned, the private law proposals of the Scottish Law Commission go some way towards achieving a more appropriate balance between the rights of the individual child and the autonomy of the family. If there are no obvious concerns about the welfare of a child, then it is probably in accord with the UN Convention on the Rights of the Child to proceed on the basis that parents are primarily responsible for making arrangements for their children. Support would seem to be more appropriate than policing. Having said that, Richards (1994) asserts that:

> *...it is important to acknowledge that the interests of parents and children (and not just those between the parents) may diverge at divorce.*

If the law really wants to achieve a proper balance between the rights of children and the responsibility of the parents, it must provide substantial support in the form of mediation services which promote a resolution of issues which best serve the interests of the child. These should incorporate a counselling service to help children to identify their feelings and articulate any views they wish to be fed into the process. If mediation fails and the matter is brought to court, then we cannot act upon the presumption that parents best represent the interests of their children, because these very parents are in disagreement about where the interests of the children lie. It is submitted that, in such proceedings, there should always be an independent person representing the interests of the child. If a mature child disagrees with the recommendations put forward by that person, then there should be a possibility of independent legal representation of that child. Maturity is a concept recognised in the Convention on the Rights of the Child as affecting the weight to be given to a child's opinion (Article 12). The Scottish Law Commission (1992) recommended that:

> *It should presumed that a child of or above the age of 12 years is capable of forming his or her own views and has sufficient maturity to express a reasonable view.* (Rec.34(c).)

The Scottish Law Commission proposals would certainly help, but they need to be backed up by supportive services. These must ensure that the system facilitates implementation of the principle of taking children's wishes into account, and picks up those children who may have wishes which should be put before the court.

The White Paper on public child welfare law also goes some way towards achieving a better balance of rights. The widening of Section 12 is welcome, as are the proposals to allow children to speak privately to the hearing, and the renewed emphasis on Safeguarders.

However, the proposals do not go far enough. The tension between the rights of the child and the rights of the parents is referred to, but its implications are not fully explored. At the time of writing, the outcome of the Scottish Office's review of the role and functions of Safeguarders is awaited. It is hoped that its conclusions will reflect a reversal of the presumption that parents in child protection cases are the most appropriate persons to represent the interests of their children.

Neither of these sets of proposals addresses the issue of the ambivalence in the policing/supportive role of the social worker. Nor would one expect them to. It is a question related more to management issues and the structure of the social work profession. The latter was the subject of extensive comment by Lord Clyde in the Orkney Report. Great emphasis was laid on the need to provide more extensive basic and post-qualifying training for social workers. It was recognised that there was a need to promote debate on 'the role and function of social work as a profession for the future so as best to serve the needs of the community.' It was suggested that:

ADSW (Association of Directors of Social Work) should consider the taking of appropriate initiatives to develop a centralised self-governing profession of social worker in Scotland. (Rec.169.)

This was followed by a recommendation that:

The whole area of work in child protection requires to be seen as a specialist area to be undertaken by practitioners with specialist skills and knowledge with adequate training and support. (Rec.170.)

Conclusion

Perhaps what is needed to address these issues further is a new set of names and designations to reflect the differing roles, responsibilities and expertise of the various people who now call themselves social workers. The widening of positive support through a new Section 12 could be the province of non-specialist social workers – community social workers – who would have no greater duties to make enquiries under Section 37 of the 1968 Act than other adults, including teachers, who come into contact with children; who are, in one sense, 'spies', as all concerned adults should be, but who are not 'detectives.'

Social work values would tend to emphasise the 'caring and supportive' role spoken of by Lord Clyde, and to disavow any role as 'spies or detectives.' They would also tend to shrink from the professional elitism suggested by reorganisation as a self-governing profession with a demanding level of entry.

Nevertheless, justice requires that authority, responsibility, expertise and intervention be recognised for what they are. Legal structures, professional structures and professional practice must be built upon principles which acknowledge the healthy tension between supportive and policing roles, rather than upon hidden, or feared and unacknowledged, conflict.

Returning to the three key sets of principles contained in the UN Convention on the Rights of the Child, it is suggested that acknowledgement of this tension in the three areas could be achieved:

- in **participation** by retaining, as a general principle in matters of private law, the presumption that parents are the best advocates for their children, but at the same time setting in place structures to help identify and address those children for whom the presumption does not hold
- in **protection** by reversing the presumption that parents involved in proceedings relating to compulsory care are the best advocates for their children

- in **provision** by the establishment of a restructured, self-governing social work profession, which matches authority, responsibility and expertise with a public acknowledgement of the status of the professionals concerned.

References

Clyde Report (1992) *Report of the Inquiry into the Removal of Children from Orkney in February 1991.* Edinburgh: HMSO.

Duquette D. (1994) Scottish children's hearings and representation for the child, in S. Asquith and M. Hill *Justice for Children.* Dordrecht, Martinus Nijhoff.

General Assembly of the United Nations (1989) *The Convention on the Rights of the Child.*

Gibbons J. (1990), with Thorpe S. and Wilkinson P. *Family Support and Prevention: Studies in Local Areas.* London: HMSO.

Kearney B. and Mapstone E. (1992) *The Report of the Inquiry into Child Care Policies in Fife.* Edinburgh: HMSO.

Kilbrandon (1964) *Children and Young Persons: Scotland.* Cmnd 2306

Lockyer A. (1994) The Scottish children's hearings system, in S. Asquith and M. Hill *Justice for Children.* Dordrecht, Martinus Nijhoff.

Scottish Law Commission (1992) *Report on Family Law.* Edinburgh: HMSO.

Scottish Office (1993) *Scotland's Children – Proposals for Child Care Policy and Law.* White Paper. Edinburgh: HMSO.

Scottish Office (1994) *Scotland's Children – Speaking Out – Young People's Views on Child Care Law in Scotland.* Edinburgh: HMSO.

Sutherland E. (1991) The role of children in the making of decisions which affect them, in M. Freeman and P. Veerman *The Ideologies of Children's Rights.* Netherlands: Kluwer.

Richards M. (1994) *The Interests of Children at Divorce.* Paper given at Family Mediation Conference, Edinburgh, 3/10/94, but originally presented at an International Conference, 'Families and Justice', Brussels, July 1994).

6

FAMILY SUPPORT IN CHILD PROTECTION

Jane Gibbons

IN this chapter I shall consider two aspects of the relationship between family support and child protection. First I consider the case for re-balancing priorities between child protection investigative procedures on the one hand and the provision of family support services to children in need on the other. The second issue concerns the nature and effectiveness of the supportive provision made for children who have experienced maltreatment.

Definitions

The concepts 'family support' and 'child protection' are difficult to define precisely. They may be used by different people in different ways, so that arguments easily become confused. For the purposes of this chapter, which has an English author, the terms will be understood by reference to the Children Act (1989) and associated guidance from the Department of Health in London.

Part III of the Children Act lays on local authorities in England and Wales a general duty to safeguard and promote the welfare of children in need and to promote the upbringing of such children within their own families (where this is in the child's interests). A child is taken to be 'in need' if:

- he is unlikely to achieve or maintain, or to have the opportunity of achieving or maintaining, a reasonable standard of health or development without the provision for him of services by a local authority;
- his health or development is likely to be severely impaired, or further impaired, without the provision for him of such services; or
- he is disabled (Section 17(10)).

Under the 1980 Child Care Act local authorities had the power to provide supportive services in order to prevent reception into care. The Children Act 1989 placed more emphasis on the positive promotion of welfare. In its Guidance the Department of Health stressed the breadth of the concept of 'need'.

> *The definition of need...is deliberately wide to reinforce the emphasis on preventive support and services to families. It has three categories: a*

reasonable standard of health or development; significant impairment of health or development; and disablement. It would not be acceptable for an authority to exclude any of these three – for example by confining services to children at risk of significant harm. (DoH, 1991, para 2.4.)

Local authorities must ensure that a range of services is available to meet the extent and nature of need identified within their administrative boundaries. Such services include, for example, day-care provision for pre-school and school-aged children, services to support and improve the strengths of parents within their own homes, advice services, material help and family centres. Local authorities must work in partnership with other providers. They must publicise the range of family support available as well as undertake monitoring and evaluation.

The term 'family support services' will in this chapter be taken to refer to the type of services which local authorities have a duty to provide or purchase for the purpose of promoting the welfare of children in need, wherever possible in their own homes.

The Children Act (1989) also lays on local authorities a specific duty to carry out enquiries when there is reasonable cause to suspect that a child in the area is suffering, or is likely to suffer, significant harm. Authorities must make or cause to be made 'such enquiries as they consider necessary to enable them to decide whether they should take any action to safeguard or promote the child's welfare' (Section 47(1)). Inter-departmental Guidance, *Working Together Under the Children Act 1989* further elaborates this duty by specifying procedures to be followed by local agencies, co-ordinated through multi-agency Area Child Protection Committees (Home Office et al., 1991). The Guidance places more emphasis than does the Children Act itself on 'protection' and the detailed steps in 'investigation', not pursuing the possibilities of a broader approach suggested by the Act's wording – 'enquire' and 'safeguard and promote welfare'. It would be a reckless local authority, however, that disregarded the Guidance on investigative procedures especially since it has been translated into performance indicators which are the basis for inspections (Social Services Inspectorate, 1993).

Tensions between protection and support

There appears to be an inherent tension between the general duty to promote the welfare of children in need in a particular area and the specific duty to target resources towards children in need of protection from significant harm. Research into the implementation of the Children Act demonstrated that the overwhelming majority of local authorities in England were continuing to give priority to the children for whom they already had some responsibility, with children at risk of abuse or neglect and children in care or accommodation ranked highest. Some support was being provided to families below the threshold for full child protection procedures, but it was likely to be subordinate to the demands of child protection work and such families had to be exceptionally demanding and persistent to get help (Department of Health, 1993). So far at least, the new approach to family support expressed in the Children Act appears not to have had a great deal of influence on the policies and practices of English local authorities.

Research into local authority services for children provides further illustration of the dominance of protection. In a study set in eight English local authorities in the early 1990s, during a 16 week period social workers notified all referrals that raised child protection concerns considered to require investigation (Gibbons et al., 1994). The researchers tracked the referrals using case records and identified a number of 'filters' – decision points when cases were extruded from the child protection process without needing to be placed on a child protection register. Table 1 illustrates the operation of these filters, showing that fewer than one in four of the cases referred for investigation reached an initial child protection conference, and fewer than one in five were placed on the child protection register. The children who were thus ejected from the system probably had no need for specific protection but, in most cases, they were living in severely deprived circumstances in families with many problems. They appeared to fit within the Children Act's definition of 'need', making them eligible for family support services but these were rarely offered. The most common outcome was case closure without any services being provided. The assessments of

Table 1. Operation of filters in child protection systems of 8 English local authorities

ENTRY POINT	IN SYSTEM	FILTERED OUT
New Incident	1,888 cases ——>	42 'lost' cases
FIRST FILTER Checks only	1,846 (100%) ——>	478 (26%)
SECOND FILTER Further investigation	1,368 (74%) ——>	925 (50%)
THIRD FILTER Initial CP Conference	443 (24%) ——>	128 (7%)
RETAINED IN SYSTEM AFTER CONFERENCE	315 (17%)	
OF WHOM: **ON REGISTER**	272 (15%)	

social workers were narrowly focused on the child protection issue and other needs tended to be ignored.

In its recent study of child health and social services provision for children in need the Audit Commission (1994) was critical of the failure of both health and social services authorities to develop co-ordinated approaches to identifying local needs and priorities, failure to clarify objectives and assess outcomes of services that are provided and failure to collaborate in the provision of family support. The report questioned the dominating role of reactive child protection investigation in social services and recommended a broader approach:

> *Traditionally, most child care cases have been channelled to social workers, who have acted as 'gatekeepers' for more specialised services. Following the Children Act social services have wider responsibilities – requiring a broader approach which may at times not necessarily involve social workers at all. This broader approach allows the diversion of some families to other resources, providing a more proactive service that makes use of a wider range of options* (Audit Commission, 1994, paras 127–128).

The broader approach to needs advocated by the Commission involves 're-balancing' children and families' work – investing more in 'universal' provision such as playgroups, childminding and the development of a range of alternative community support resources.

Needs of children who have experienced maltreatment

So far this chapter has developed the argument that the concentration of resources in children and families' services on child protection, in particular on investigations which in the majority of cases are unproductive, has prevented the policy shift towards the promotion of welfare promised by the Children Act. However, this is not to deny the needs of maltreated children for help. Research into the operation of child protection registers, already referred to, produced crude indicators of the high level of needs among children placed on the register for different forms of maltreatment (Table 2). The majority of families lacked a wage-earner, many had severe financial problems and were in insecure housing. In over half the cases there had been previous investigations for child abuse. Violence between the adults in the household was common as were other parental difficulties. Other surveys have confirmed that children placed on protection registers in Britain are likely to be living in conditions of severe disadvantage. They will often be exposed to styles of parenting which will adversely affect their development (Gough et al., 1987; Creighton & Noyes, 1989).

The evidence from longitudinal studies of the longer-term specific effects of maltreatment upon children's development is conflicting. In the case of physical abuse it is likely that only the very few cases of severe injury

Table 2. Family characteristics of children on protection registers in 8 English local authorities

Characteristic	Neglect (N=27) % cases on register	Physical Abuse (N=119) % cases on register	Sexual Abuse (N=82) % cases on register
Dependent on Social Security	96	51	61
Homeless/Temporary Accommodation	23	15	6
Debts Mentioned in Record	89	35	31
Previous Abuse Investigation	67	53	47
Parent Substance Abuse	67	25	18
Parent Criminal Record	44	33	32
Parent Mental Illness	30	22	15
Violence Between Partners	37	51	29

resulting in brain damage will leave lasting, specific effects upon children's physical and cognitive development. However, children who were physically maltreated in early life probably show more behaviour problems at home and school, are less happy and successful and have more troubled relationships than other children, even when social class factors are controlled (Gibbons & Gallagher, 1993). Such children appear to have higher chances of being arrested for juvenile delinquency and adult crime in later life (Widom, 1989). Although neglect is seen as a chronic, low-risk state of affairs, it may produce as many fatalities as does physical abuse, due to accidents (Margolin, 1990). There may also be serious effects on children's cognitive and emotional development (Egeland et al., 1983; Wodarski et al., 1990; Claussen and Crittenden, 1991). Sexually abused children may suffer long-lasting effects on their self-esteem and emotional health (Browne & Finkelhor, 1986).

Maltreated children, therefore, have a strong case to be early in the queue for access to compensatory services. It would seem that services geared to assisting parents to overcome their own problems (such as alcohol and drug abuse) and to increase family income by gaining new skills and possibilities of employment may be as important as services intended to improve parenting skills and family relationships. Many children need help with handling the demands of school and with the social skills needed to make and maintain friendships. Violence in the families of maltreated children is widespread – affecting adult relationships and styles of parenting. Anti-violence strategies therefore should be a priority in developing compensatory services for children. Physical ill-treatment may be indicative of a general style of parenting – lacking in warmth and consistency, excessively critical and reliant on physical punishment – that is harmful. Such parenting methods can be addressed in compensatory services.

Service provision for maltreated children

There is a surprisingly little good evidence on the services actually received by maltreated children placed on protection registers. Using case records, Corby (1987) followed up 25 families for two years after a child protection conference and interviewed ten of them. He found a general absence of formal assessment of the families' needs and functioning. Perhaps related to this lack, the usual service consisted of general 'support', combined with indirect monitoring through other agencies, such as nurseries and health visitors. These were aware of their primary checking function and would have preferred more openness about it. Corby and Mills (1986) identified various strategies adopted by key workers, ranging from minimal further action, through low-level and more intensive monitoring combined with support, up to removal of the child from home.

Gough et al. (1987) studied 29 cases of children who had been placed on Scottish registers after injury and identified six categories of case management according to the degree of control applied. They concluded that the system was based on ensuring that a basic minimum of care was being provided, rather than on detailed analysis of the adults' motivations and parenting abilities. More specific help to address children's difficulties was rarely provided. Other professions such as medicine only had a narrow, specialised role within the social worker's case management and were seldom involved even in that sphere.

Gibbons et al. (1994) followed up 399 children for 26 weeks after a child protection conference by examining case records. Two-thirds of the children were on the child protection register. Four patterns of service delivery were described. In *low provision* there was no legal intervention and no offer of supportive services. Only a quarter of cases on the register experienced this compared with about half the cases that were not registered at the conference. The *supportive* pattern involved no legal intervention but the provision of some supportive service and was the most commonly found in both registered and non-registered cases. *Controlling support* combined legal intervention and supportive provision. It was used in a fifth of cases on the register but in only 4% of cases not registered. *Enforcement* consisted of legal actions without any supportive provision and was uncommon – found in about 5% of registered and non-registered cases. Thus control through legal means was not necessary in about three-quarters of cases on the register.

In this study the most common form of supportive service consisted of financial or practical help, usually small amounts of money or goods to help in family crises. Few children on the register received help from a child psychiatrist (13%) or other counselling help (6%). Even fewer received assistance with learning or other school problems. Referrals to family centres were unusual (8%) and hardly any families were linked to voluntary sources of support. However this study demonstrated that social workers were highly conscientious in their monitoring of families where children were on the register, maintaining regular contact over the follow-up period.

Farmer and Owen (1993) followed up 44 children who had been placed on registers in England. They concluded that the priority given to the child's protection meant that little attention was given to broader welfare issues. A child's disturbed behaviour or even a family's impending homelessness could be seen as outside the caseworker's 'protective' remit. Treatment needs of disturbed and depressed children were sometimes overlooked.

The recent British research, therefore, is consistent in finding that 'protection', narrowly understood, is the dominating concern in work with maltreated children and their families, while assessment of needs and provision of compensatory supportive services are relegated to a less important or even marginal role. The balance between protection and family support may need re-adjustment at this end of the child protection system as well as in the early stages.

Shifting the balance towards family support

Children who experience maltreatment are best seen as 'children first': they do not form a homogeneous group nor do they all have needs that cannot be met through existing forms of provision. However, family support provision cannot compensate for primary poverty, as the gap between rich and poor families widens (Department of Social Security, 1992; see chapter 4 by Long in this volume).

In terms of service provision, maltreated children first of all need access (perhaps preferential access) to health and educational provision that is universally available. Second, while all children should have access to good quality early years daycare and education, children from poor families with special needs may benefit most. In the USA long-term follow-up studies of disadvantaged black children who attended the Perry Pre-School Programme showed that, by comparison with similar children who did not attend, in later life they achieved better literacy and better jobs, they were less likely to be arrested and less likely to have early pregnancies

(Schweinhart & Weikhart, 1993). The components of effective pre-school provision identified in the research were:

- a curriculum which allows children to choose educational activities within a structured framework
- involving parents as partners in the programme and visiting parents at home
- teachers with training in child development
- small classes
- staff development and support
- close links with infant and primary school provision.

The development of pre-school provision is needed for all under-fives, but maltreated children and their families are likely to gain more than most from high-quality, intensive provision that involves parents as active participants. At present, while the majority of pre-school children on child protection registers are probably given day nursery places, the purpose is often to monitor the child's safety and provide basic care. The quality of the provision in educational terms is not always considered.

'Special needs' provision

Some family support services have a bias towards families facing more difficulties, although they are not specifically geared towards child maltreatment. Particularly helpful are family projects that are located within the neighbourhood they serve, often with local management and with a strong volunteer or para-professional component. In this type of project, which may be funded by voluntary bodies, the government or local authorities, the paid staff have no statutory duties, there are usually few formalities or bureaucratic procedures and there is little social distance between staff and users – indeed a recipient of help may also be giving it. There may be less stigma attached to such projects than there is to social service departments or clinics. Costs are likely to be lower, although training, supervision and support and management all impose significant costs.

Evaluative research, comprehensively reviewed by David Gough (1993), has been carried out on a number of such projects. Home-Start is a well-established volunteer scheme that operates throughout most of Britain. Parent volunteers in each locally managed scheme are matched with mothers who are having problems in bringing up their young children. Paid organisers are responsible for recruitment, training and supervising the volunteers, who visit families at home, attempt to establish supportive friendships and link mothers to other community resources. Evaluative research found that volunteers were able to help families who resembled clients of social services departments on various measures of need and risk. Compared to social workers, volunteers spent much more time with families and engaged in more family support activities. Parents who had Home-Start volunteers were significantly more satisfied with their help than were social workers' clients. In uncontrolled research, positive outcomes have been found in the majority of Home-Start families (Van der Eyken, 1982; Gibbons & Thorpe, 1989).

Newpin, a befriending scheme and therapeutic network, was founded in South London in 1980 and has spread to a number of other areas. Newpin has a particular remit to prevent child abuse. It takes referrals mainly from health visitors and social workers. Clients consist mainly of women with long-standing mental health problems and familes in exceptionally adverse circumstances. Newpin provides a drop-in centre, a programme of activities and crafts and a befriending programme in which users graduate through a training programme to act as volunteers. A further course prepares volunteers to take on the responsibilities of a project co-ordinator. Evaluation showed that 70% of mothers who joined the scheme maintained their involvement and that mothers in the greatest adversity were most likely to continue. Those who continued showed striking improvements in self-esteem and control over their lives. The greatest improvement occurred between seven and twelve months involvement, whereas little change occurred in the short-term – less than six months. There were fewer changes in parent/child relationships and mothers' styles of parenting as assessed by independent observational measures, but mothers became more able to anticipate their children's needs (Cox et al., 1992).

Early intervention

Another group of studies has examined early intervention programmes for broadly-defined 'high-risk' groups. The components of these programmes included more intensive services from health visitors or community nurses, practical and educational help and social support. Olds et al. (1986a, 1986b, 1988), for example, reported on a random allocation experiment in which 400 mothers-to-be who were considered to be 'at risk' were assigned to different intervention groups. Mothers who received developmental screening plus transport and home visiting during and after pregnancy fared better on outcome measures than those who had screening only or just screening combined with free transport. There were significant effects on diet, support systems and smoking. Treatment groups had fewer parenting problems and made fewer hospital visits. Barth (1991) studied outcomes of the Child Parent Enrichment Project (CPEP) in the USA. Trained para-professional parenting consultants made on average eleven home visits during a six-month period to pregnant women who were identified as having at least two 'risk factors'. A control group received routine health or social services. Consultants worked in a task-centred way on parenting skills and also provided practical help. Although parents receiving the special service were satisfied with its help, there were few advantages on more objective measures such as child abuse reports and access to sources of support. It may be, as the Newpin research would suggest, that the time period of service was too short.

In reviewing a large number of studies of early intervention in high risk groups Gough (1993) concluded that the costs of the interventions were high considering the weak evidence of the modest results so far achieved. However, the results of specialist treatment programmes are also far from clear-cut and, as Gough stated, 'the most rigorous experimental designs report the least encouraging results'.

Direct work with children

There are few reports of compensatory services aimed specifically at maltreated children, rather than primarily at families or parents. Culp and colleagues (1987) evaluated the programme at a therapeutic day centre for physically abused and neglected pre-school children. The children spent six hours a day in groups, receiving play therapy, speech and occupational therapy and special education. Nutritious meals were provided. Parents were closely involved in the programme. The children were assessed on measures of language, motor skills and self-care before and after taking part in the programme. Girls made greater gains than boys on all the measures and abused children gained more than neglected children, who were felt to be too distractible to benefit from the structured teaching environment.

A different approach was evaluated by Fantuzzo (1988). The Mount Hope Family Center in the USA provided a special service intended to increase the positive social behaviour of withdrawn, maltreated pre-school children. Children functioning well in the day center program were chosen to act as 'balancers' in play therapy for poorly functioning children who had experienced (or were at risk of) physical abuse or neglect. The 'confederate' children were trained through games and role play to encourage the withdrawn children to engage in play and social interaction. Ratings of change were based on observational measures. The results suggested that the 'balancing' children were effective in increasing prosocial behaviour and responsiveness among the withdrawn group. In contrast, a comparison group of abused children placed with adults who initiated play performed worse. Perhaps malteated children learn to be wary of adults but find it easier to respond to peers. It would be interesting to develop the ideas guiding this programme in work with older children and also with maltreated children who are not withdrawn but who antagonise their peers through uncontrolled and over-demanding behaviour.

Conclusions

Over the last two decades the balance in services for children and families has tilted away from the promotion of welfare and the development of effective family support services towards the identification of children at risk and the development of procedures for their surveillance (Parton, 1991). Arrangements originally devised to protect a small group of severely injured infants have come to be used for a much wider group of children living in adverse conditions. The Children Act (1989) has made it necessary for local authorities to re-assess priorities and tilt the balance towards family support. Within broadly based services for children and families it is vital to retain protective services for children who have been seriously injured or assaulted or have experienced extreme and demonstrably damaging neglect. However it is unlikely that such events can be predicted in advance. Subjecting large numbers of children living in unsatisfactory conditions to screening for significant harm (as happens under present child protective procedures) is unlikely to prevent serious assault or death in the future.

Investment in universal educational and health services (including good quality pre-school provision) and ensuring that children in need obtain access to it is a better strategy. Neighbourhoods containing many such children may benefit from locally based family projects. Some compensatory services with more specific educational or therapeutic goals may also have a role to play if independent evaluation confirms their value.

References

Audit Commission (1994) *Seen but not Heard: Co-ordinating Community Child Health and Social Services for Children in Need*. London: HMSO.

Barth, R.P (1991) An experimental evaluation of an in-house child abuse prevention service. *Child Abuse & Neglect*, 15, 363–375.

Browne, A. & Finkelhor D. (1986) The impact of child sexual abuse: a review of the research. *Psychological Bulletin*, 99, 66–77

Claussen, A.H. and Crittenden, P.M. (1991) Physical and psychological maltreatment: relation among types of maltreatment. *Child Abuse & Neglect*, 15, 5–18.

Corby, B. (1987) *Working with Child Abuse*. Milton Keynes: Open University Press.

Corby, B. and Mills, C. (1986) Child abuse: risks and resources. *British Journal of Social Work*, 16, 531-542.

Cox, A., Pound, A. and Pickering, C. (1992) Newpin: A befriending scheme and therapeutic network for carers of young children. In J. Gibbons (ed.) *The Children Act 1989 and Family Support: Principles into Practice*. London: HMSO.

Creighton, S.J. and Noyes, P. (1989) *Child Abuse Trends in England and Wales 1983–1987*. London: National Society for the Prevention of Cruelty to Children.

Culp, R.E., Richardson, M.T. and Heide, J.S. (1987) Differential developmental progress of maltreated children in day treatment. *Social Work*, 32, 497–499.

Department of Health (1991) *The Children Act 1989 Guidance and Regulations: Vol. 2: Family support, day care and educational provision for young children.* London: HMSO.
Department of Health (1994) *Children Act Report 1993.* London: HMSO.
Department of Social Security (1992) *Households Below Average Income: A Statistical Analysis.* London: HMSO.
Egeland, B., Sroufe, A. and Erickson, M.A. (1983) Developmental consequences of different patterns of maltreatment. *Child Abuse & Neglect,* 7, 459–469.
Fantuzzo, J.W., Jurecic, L., Stovall, A. et al., (1988) Effects of adult and peer social initiations on the social behaviour of withdrawn, maltreated pre-school children. *Journal of Consulting and Clinical Psychology,* 56, 34–39.
Farmer, E. and Owen, M. (1993) *Decision-Making, Intervention and Outcome in Child Protection Work.* University of Bristol: Report to Department of Health.
Gibbons, J. and Thorpe, S. (1989) Can voluntary support projects help vulnerable families? The work of Home-Start. *British Journal of Social Work,* 19, 189–201.
Gibbons, J. and Gallagher, B. (1993) *Development of Children after Physical Abuse in Early Life: Report to Department of Health.* University of East Anglia.
Gibbons, J., Conroy, S. and Bell, C. (1994) *Operating the Child Protection System.* London: HMSO.
Gough, D. (1993) *Child Abuse Interventions: A review of the research literature.* London: HMSO.
Gough, D.A., Body, F.A., Dunning, N. and Stone, F.H. (1987) *A Longitudinal Study of Child Abuse in Glasgow.* University of Glasgow and Greater Glasgow Health Board.
Home Office, Department of Health, Department of Education and Science and Welsh Office (1991) *Working Together Under the Children Act 1989.* London: HMSO.
Margolin, L. (1990) Fatal child neglect. *Child Welfare,* 69, 309–319.
Olds, D., Henderson, C.R., Tatelbaum, R. and Chamberlain, R. (1986a) Improving the delivery of prenatal care and outcome of pregnancy. *Pediatrics,* 77, 16–28.
Olds, D., Henderson, C.R., Chamberlain, R. and Tatelbaum, R. (1986b) Preventing child abuse and neglect: a randomized trial of nurse home visits. *Pediatrics,* 78, 65–78.
Olds, D., Henderson, C.R., Tatelbaum, R. and Chamberlain, R. (1988) Improving the life course development of socially disadvantaged mothers: a randomized trial of nurse home visits. *American Journal of Public Health,* 78, 1436–1445.
Parton, N. (1991) *Governing the Family: Child Care, Child Protection and the State.* Basingstoke: Macmillan.
Schweinhart, L.J. and Weikart, D. (1993) *A Summary of Significant Benefits: The High/Scope Perry Preschool Study Through Age 27.* Ypsilanti Mich.: High/Scope Press.
Social Services Inspectorate (1993) *Inspecting for Quality: Evaluating Performance in Child Protection.* London: HMSO
Van der Eyken, W. (1982) *Home Start: A Four-year Evaluation.* Leicester: Home Start Consultancy.
Widom, C.S. (1989) The cycle of violence, *Science,* 244, 160–166
Wodarski, J. (1990) Maltreatment and the school-age child: major academic, socio-emotional and adaptive outcomes. *Social Work,* 35, 506–513.

7

Social Support and Early Years Centres

Rosalind Hawthorne Kirk

Introduction

The centre helps my child to learn to speak and with her education. It lets her meet other children, more than she would if we didn't come here because we live in a multi. We meet other parents, talk and chat about things and feel better after it – feel more reassured in yourself.

A SCOTTISH mother describes the impact the local family centre has on the life of her family. The preventive functions of day care and family centres have been convincingly argued (Gibbons, 1990, Holman, 1988) whilst challenges have been made that family centres can also serve to reinforce traditional home-making roles for women and do not reflect changing patterns of child rearing and family life (Kirk, 1990, Canaan, 1992).

Debate about the effectiveness and purpose of early years provision continues amidst growing knowledge and research on quality and lack of places (e.g. McGurk et al, 1993, Goldschmied and Jackson, 1994). Risks associated with day care and its impact on child outcomes have also been extensively studied (Scarr and Eisenberg, 1993).

The direct impact on parents of early years provision has been largely neglected yet it is an increasingly important area. Increasing demands for services mean that there is a need to see to what extent parental aspirations are being realised. Parental employment is only one of many diverse reasons for using early years provision. It provides development enhancing experiences for young children with their peers and other consistent, caring adults outside the immediate family. At the same time it may enable parents to take up training, develop new friendships, skills and self-confidence through participation in the centre itself, in the workplace or in community activities (Kirk, 1994). It may also provide opportunities to reduce isolation and to build an extended social support network.

This chapter describes a Scottish study that examines contrasting types of public early years provision to see what relationship, if any, they may have to the parents' social support networks, family wellbeing and the child's development. Although the study is longitudinal, this chapter is concerned with the initial phase. First, though, the wider context of early years provision will be reviewed.

Early years provision
Range and availability

There is considerable diversity in the range of early years services but this does not correspond directly with parental choice, as differences in cost and access result in segregated services because use depends on the level of parental income, knowledge of services and how to access them. Inconsistencies and ambiguities in the collection of official statistics on the levels of day care and education make comparisons between different types of services and across authorities difficult. Nevertheless, they remain the main national source of this information.

According to SCAFA (1992), in the UK, 2% of children under three and 35–40% of those from three years to school age had access to local authority day care i.e. education nursery schools and classes or social work day nurseries, family or children's centres. Nursery schools and classes and playgroups provided only part time places for three and four year olds. In Scotland, these were available for 34% of this age group in both types of facility. Childminders, day nurseries, family centres and nannies provide care for babies up to school age, although it can vary from one establishment to another which age range is catered for and whether places are full or part-time. In 1990, 1.6% of all pre-school aged children had places available in local authority day nurseries and family centres. In the private and voluntary sectors, childminders had places for 4% of the under fives while private and voluntary nurseries provided for 0.4%. The numbers of children cared for by nannies or in informal situations is not known because this area of care is largely unregulated. Care by relatives continues to be the most commonly used form of childcare. Britain continues to have one of the lowest levels of publicly funded day care in Europe (Cohen,1990; SCAFA,1992). The first statutory reviews of early years services were completed by local authorities across the country in 1992 and although there have been some increases, mainly in the private nursery sector, the demand and need for services greatly outstripped supply (Martyn,1994).

The role of central government

The role of central government in the provision of early years services has been contested over many years and has a fragmented history. The political ideologies that have been dominant over the past fifteen years, accompanied by economic recession, increased poverty, widespread unemployment and low pay, have placed increased emphasis on parental responsibilities and argued for minimal state provided welfare (Williams, 1989). This has been reflected in recent child care legislation (Children Act, 1989) which included the provision, regulation and review of early years services. It emphasised parental responsibility and the privacy of the family unless parenting is deemed inadequate or children have special needs.

In England and Wales, the Children Act, as it related to early years provision, gave prominence to the provision of day care by family centres for children 'in need'. In contrast to the integrated and far reaching nature of this piece of child care legislation, only those parts of the Act concerned with regulation and review of early years services applied in Scotland which it was hoped would be incorporated into a comprehensive piece of Scottish child care law. However, the White Paper on this, 'Scotland's Children' (1993) was disappointing and referred to day care in only very general terms. The changes brought about by the Children Act and the encouragement of a 'mixed economy' in day care were viewed as central government's contribution to early years services in Scotland, making reference to its welfare function:

> *Day care also fulfils an important preventive role by providing a range of resources from mutual self-help to parent-craft training and health education. This short or medium term intervention can serve in many instances to prevent the need for statutory intervention or reception into care at a later stage.* (p.12.)

This statement reflects the view that state intervention in family life through day care is appropriate mainly for certain inadequate individuals, usually mothers, since most of the participants in such groups are known to be women. Unlike the changes in the role of the state arising from community care legislation which promotes the rights of carers of dependent adults for support, parents of young children are not viewed as similarly in need of support. Bringing up children is a private family matter and the responsibility of parents, although it could be argued that the tasks and demands are such, and the potential benefits of providing a range of services and supports so great, that investment in day care and family support makes sense both economically and socially.

North American cost-benefit analysis of publicly funded pre-school programmes (e.g. Barnett, 1993) demonstrated that the investment of $1 by the taxpayer yielded savings of at least $7 through reducing children's needs for a wide range of health, welfare and policing services while improving educational attainment and employment prospects.

Day care as social support
'Social support' is a concept rather than a straightforward term, in much the same way as 'family'. Both are used frequently as if there is a common,

shared understanding when that is rarely the case. Social support is defined by Dunst et al, (1988) as including:

> *The emotional, physical, informational, instrumental and material aid and assistance provided by others to maintain health and well-being, promote adaptations of life events, and foster development in an adaptive manner.* (p.28.)

Sources of support include both informal support networks such as kin, friends, neighbours and social groups like clubs or churches and formal sources – professionals, agencies and organisations such as early years centres. The nature of support may be analysed according to quantitative attributes including network size, density and reciprocity, as well as qualities such as availability, source and content. Social support networks can act positively to mediate or moderate stress but can also be a source of stress when conflict arises within them. A number of factors influence the availability and use of support including personality, gender, geographical location, life changes and family variables (Krahn, 1993). Individuals' need for, and satisfaction with, support are dependent on individual coping abilities, personal life events and the wider social context in which they are helped or constrained in their abilities to put coping strategies into practice (Monat and Lazarus, 1991).

While caution should be expressed about interpreting studies on social support as inferring a direct causal link, strong correlational relationships have been found with beneficial effects on health and well-being (Cohen and Syme, 1985) and adjustment to life crises (Moos, 1986). Culbertson and Schellenbach (1992) reviewed the literature on social support and parenting and concluded that there was evidence to support a direct relationship between social support and quality of parenting. In a model proposed by Dunst et al (1988) social support is seen to influence parental well-being and health, which then impacts on family functioning and child development. They also argue strongly that personal informal support networks have powerful stress buffering and health promoting qualities that can produce much greater benefits than any formal or professional sources of support or intervention.

Alongside perspectives which view parents' social networks as contributing to coping and resilience through direct influence on child development and parent-child relationships (e.g.Cochran et al,1990; Hill, 1989), deficit-model based research has also developed, particularly in the field of child protection focusing on the negative outcomes for children associated with lack of social support (e.g. Belsky, 1984). For example, in a study which aimed to identify child abuse predictors, Chan (1994) found that mothers who had abused their children experienced significantly higher levels of parenting stress and had more children yet had access to less social support than mothers in a matched control group who had not abused their children. In a further study by Gaudin et al. (1993) it was reported that neglectful parents reported more life stresses, greater depression and loneliness and weaker informal social supports than non-neglectful parents.

A study by Garbarino and Sherman (1980) on high risk neighbourhoods and high risk families approached the same issue by looking at it within the wider community context. Deccio et al. (1994) replicated this work and supported their findings which demonstrated a significant association between low income and the risk of child abuse, but not the one they had found between lack of social support and risk.

In a study of the effectiveness of contrasting styles of delivering social services in two neighbourhoods, Gibbons (1990) compared the social support systems of families who were referred clients and those who were not. She found that the numbers of supporters were the same for both groups. However, the referred families depended more on friends and professionals than family, they expressed more need for support and less satisfaction with the support they did receive. They were also more likely to view their close family as those with whom they would be in conflict. Gibbons also looked at the impact of different types of social support on abilities to cope with problems:

The availability of people to give practical help with money, childcare and other domestic tasks appeared to be important in reducing personal stress caused by high levels of family problems. (p.117.)

This study also showed the positive influence of informal help and day care for families with under fives who were experiencing parenting difficulties:

The evidence suggested that the support of family, friends and neighbours, and the use of day care provision, might have been as or more important than the help received from social services or from organised community groups. (p.149.)

Cochran et al. (1990) consider it an important gap in our knowledge and understanding that no known study contrasts the effectiveness of different models of intervention which can extend parent's social support networks:

There are cases in which network change has been used to assess the impact of a social intervention, but I know of no network studies in which institutions with the same assigned purpose, but organised differently, are compared as contexts for network building and maintenance. (p.33.)

Design of study on social support and early years centres

Early years centres, such as nursery schools, day nurseries and family centres, all aim to provide care and education opportunities which promote the development of young children and offer practical support to parents, yet they are each organised very differently. The underpinning philosophies differ, whilst the qualifications and conditions of employment of their staff vary significantly. The impact these differences may have on families is not known. A study was set up in a Scottish Regional Authority to investigate further the inter-relationships between the family, social support and local authority early years services. It aimed to find out :

- whether families with different needs are more or less likely to use particular types of centres
- how staff and users perceived the centres' support function
- whether social support had an impact on the quality of life for the parent and child in terms of outcomes such as health, levels of parenting stress and the child's development.

An ecological framework (Bronfenbrenner, 1979) was applied, drawing on the experiences of evaluating family support programmes in the USA (Weiss and Jacobs, 1988). Parental change resulting from support programmes has been said to take between one and two years (Harman and Brim, 1980). In recognition of this, the study was longitudinal over a period of a year. This necessitated data collection from a number of sources, repeated at a follow up period of a year, including demographic and employment information about the area. A number of standardised measures of general health, parenting stress, social support, child development and the pre-school environment were used in addition to interviews with the primary caregiver. Questionnaires and interviews were also completed by heads or managers of the centres.

The area

The study area (population 17,908) was located on the periphery of a major urban centre (population 165,873). It displayed some of the most extreme features of social and economic disadvantage. As a consequence of considerable investment by the authorities over recent years, the community had access to a relatively high level of low cost or free public provision of various types. There were 14 public and voluntary early years centres in the area but no private sector provision.

The 1991 census showed that 28% of households in the Region included dependent children, while 39% of the households in the study area did so. The number of young children (under five) comprised around 10% of the local population. Of these, one in three lived in lone parent households. Over half of these were without central heating and even fewer had a car (14%). The homogeneity of the sample sharing a similar physical environment meant that there were few important differences as regards socio-economic status and ethnic origin.

The centres

The study focused on local authority provision because it was thought that increased understanding of the respective roles and responsibilities of education and social work might assist in the development of a more co-ordinated approach to the provision of early years services. While boundaries between different forms of centre-based provision have become increasingly blurred, some key features can be identified which distinguished the main kinds of centres in the Region in which this study was based. Nursery schools and classes were the most commonly available type of service locally but there were also a number of family centres. Children's or family centres have become increasingly common in local authorities, alongside traditional day nursery provision. Most of them evolved from day nurseries, surplus residential provision or from inclusion of Urban programme partnerships into mainstream local authority funding. They often aim to meet the developmental needs of children as well as those of their parents for advice, information and support through the provision of a wide range of services and activities. Some have day care as a core function, while others do not and emphasise family support.

Holman (1988) described three main models of family centres as client-focused, neighbourhood and community development. The distinctions he made were useful in the context of this study. Client-focused centres, in which professionals have responsibity for determining the nature of intensive services and referral of vulnerable families, now predominate in social work and social services early years provision. This model is often viewed as most compatible with the objectives and philosophies inherent in child protection work as it enables the monitoring of families perceived to be at risk (Cannan, 1992). Neighbourhood centres, in contrast, are open to all local families and provide services and activities in response to expressed needs. They are run by professionals in partnership with users and are less common outside the voluntary sector. Community development family centres, run by and for local residents, are rare (Pennycook,1991).

The key features of the centres in this study are outlined overleaf (Table 1). Six centres were selected for participation in the study, representing three different models of early years centres – two types of family centres (client-focused and neighbourhood) and an education nursery school/class. Each model was represented by two centres.

Table 1. Features of provision.

Features	Types of centre		
	Neighbourhood family centre (NFC)	Client-focused family centre (CFC)	Nursery school or class (Nursery)
Management	Multi-agency	Social work	Education
Primary function	Family support and community development	Care and education for under fives and family support	Care and education for under fives.
Percentage places (0-5yrs) available Regionally	0.5%	2%	14.5%
Cost	Free	Means tested	Free
Parental participation	Fundamental to operation	Encouraged & required in some cases	Peripheral to operation
Hours	9-5pm, plus some evenings	8pm-6pm	9-3.30pm

The sample

An overall sample of 85 family households (representing 331 individuals) participated from a potential population of 116 families whose children were under four years of age and already attending the centres concerned (73.3% response rate). Each family was identified from the centre registers. The mean age of children included in the sample was 2.7 years, ranging from six months to three years. Age restrictions on eligibility for the education nurseries meant that all of the younger children came from the family centres and although it was initially thought preferable to restrict the sample on the basis of a single year of birth this would have limited the sample size and decreased the opportunity to explore movements between centres.

Findings

Age and ethnicity

Although there were small age differences amongst the children using centres, there were no significant differences in the age of carers across centres. The majority of female carers and fathers, where resident in the household, were under 30 years of age. 44% of the mothers in this sample had been aged 15–19 years when they had their first child, compared with only 9% of births in the general population to mothers in that age range (CSO, 1993). Proportionately more younger first time mothers attended family centres than nurseries. The population surrounding the centres comprised 0.5% of ethnic minority origin (1991 census). Only 2 of these families fell into the sample population and they used one particular centre, a client-focused family centre.

Poverty

(a) Households

The household sizes ranged from two to ten persons, with an average of two children per household. Almost a third (29%) were lone parent households and these were headed by women in all but two families. This contrasted with the national average of 18% of households with dependent children in the same year (CSO,1993). Proportionately more lone parents used the client focused family centre than other types of centre (See Figure 1).

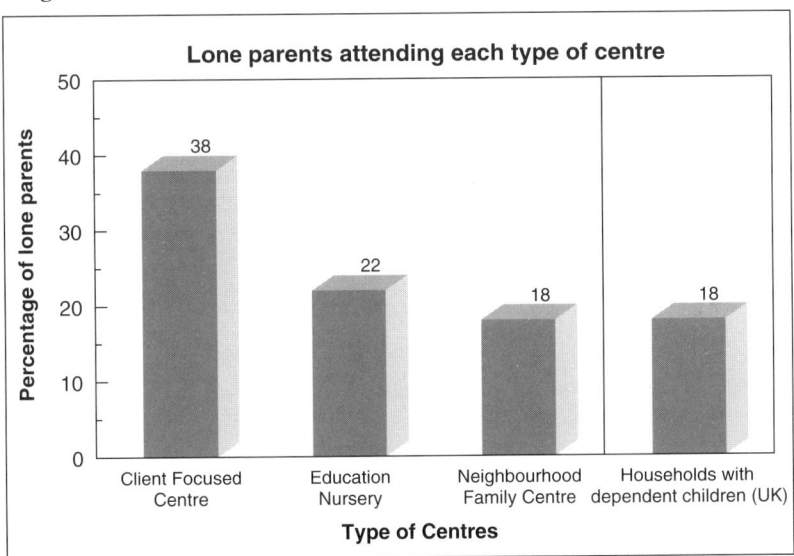

Figure 1

Lone parents attending each type of centre

Type of Centre	Percentage of lone parents
Client Focused Centre	38
Education Nursery	22
Neighbourhood Family Centre	18
Households with dependent children (UK)	18

(b) Employment and Qualifications

While 40% of women in the UK with children under five were in employment in 1991, with 29% working full time (FPSC, 1993), only 27% of those who used the centres in the study were in paid work and this was mostly part-time, casual or seasonal. The jobs also usually involved manual, unskilled work (e.g. cleaning, shop work). Ironically, the only type of centre which could provide full time care, the client focused centre, had the lowest proportion of working parents. These figures may reflect the primary functions of the centres and the restricted opportunities for work in the area rather than the needs of parents to whom a job could provide an escape from poverty and an increase in self-esteem. Figure 2 illustrates the distribution of working parents attending each type of facility.

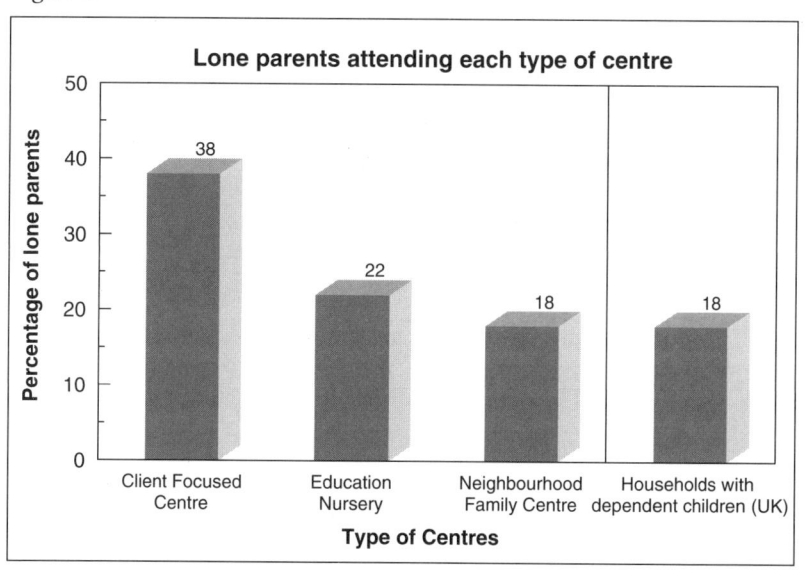

Figure 2

Lone parents attending each type of centre

Type of Centre	Percentage of lone parents
Client Focused Centre	38
Education Nursery	22
Neighbourhood Family Centre	18
Households with dependent children (UK)	18

It might be thought that the pattern of unemployment would also be reflected in the lack of qualifications held by the parents. While over half (56.5%) of all parents had no formal qualifications, just over a third (37.6%) held qualifications obtained at school such as standard grades, highers or SCOTVEC modules. The parents who had these certificates were relatively evenly distributed across all types of centres. However, the parents who had obtained a qualification through further education of some kind (6%) did not attend the nurseries but went to the family centres where rates of parental employment were lower.

Only one in five of those using client focused centres had partners in employment. This was in sharp contrast to those using nurseries and neighbourhood centres where around 50% had a partner in employment.

(c) Families' material circumstances

The distribution of household incomes (see Figure 3) showed the relative poverty of the families who used client-focused centres:

Figure 3

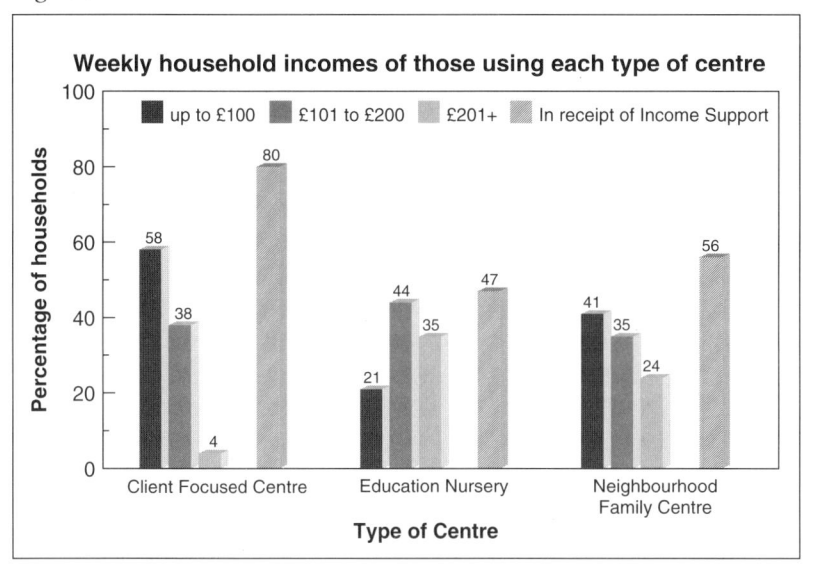

Weekly household incomes of those using each type of centre

Type of Centre	up to £100	£101 to £200	£201+	In receipt of Income Support
Client Focused Centre	58	38	4	80
Education Nursery	21	44	35	47
Neighbourhood Family Centre	41	35	24	56

Marked differences in tenancies were also found between those families who attended family centres and those who attended nursery school. While only 7% of those at family centres were owner occupiers, 35% of those using nurseries were. Similarly, families who used client-focused centres were the least likely to have a car. Only 29% had a car in comparison to around half of those who attended the other centres.

Thus the poorest families, often lone parents, attended family centres rather than nurseries, particularly client focused centres. They were also the least likely to be in paid employment or have a partner in work but they were as well, if not better, qualified than those who attended nursery. To see whether there were other characteristics which made them more likely to use family centres rather than nurseries, family well-being was investigated.

Well-being

40% of all families reported that there was a family health problem or disability. These families were equally distributed across all centres. However, this distribution was not repeated when standardised measures of parenting stress, general health and child development were analysed. The parenting stress index (Abidin, 1990) indicated that 33% of the parents had levels of parenting stress at or above that expected of 10% of parents in the general population. Over a quarter had critically high general health scores according to the General Health Questionnaire (Goldberg, 1978) pointing to the presence of health disorders in many of the parents. The same percentage had children who were assessed by a health visitor as having developmental delay, using the Schedule of Growing Skills (Bellman and Cash,1987). Figure 4 illustrates the prevalence of families in all types of centres who showed high levels of stress, poor health and those with a child showing developmental delay.

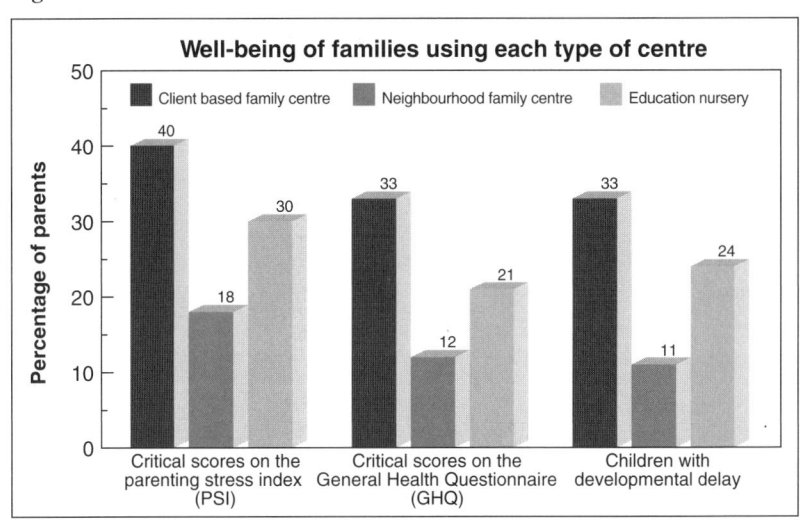

Figure 4

Well-being of families using each type of centre

	Client based family centre	Neighbourhood family centre	Education nursery
Critical scores on the parenting stress index (PSI)	40	18	30
Critical scores on the General Health Questionnaire (GHQ)	33	12	21
Children with developmental delay	33	11	24

Again, it can be seen that around a third of the families who attended client-focused centres experienced much stress and difficulty. Families who attended nursery also showed considerable pressures while those of families who went to neighbourhood centres were less so.

There were, however, differences in the length of time families had been using centres which may have been an influential factor. All parents using nurseries had done so for six months or less while this was true for around one third of family centre users. Where nearly half of those who used neighbourhood centres had been there for a year or more, only 2% of families using client focused centres had been. This will be explored at follow-up as it could be related to an optimum period of attendance for parental changes to be achieved, as mentioned earlier.

Social support networks

Almost all of the parents with critically high parenting stress and health problems identified fewer relatives in their support networks than other parents. Although all parents had some relatives who supported them, those who went to client-focused centres depended more on centre staff and other professionals, probably reflecting the fragility of their infomal support systems. Figure 5 shows the percentages of parents in different centres who identified one or more centre staff and other professionals as those who regularly provided support of various kinds.

Figure 5

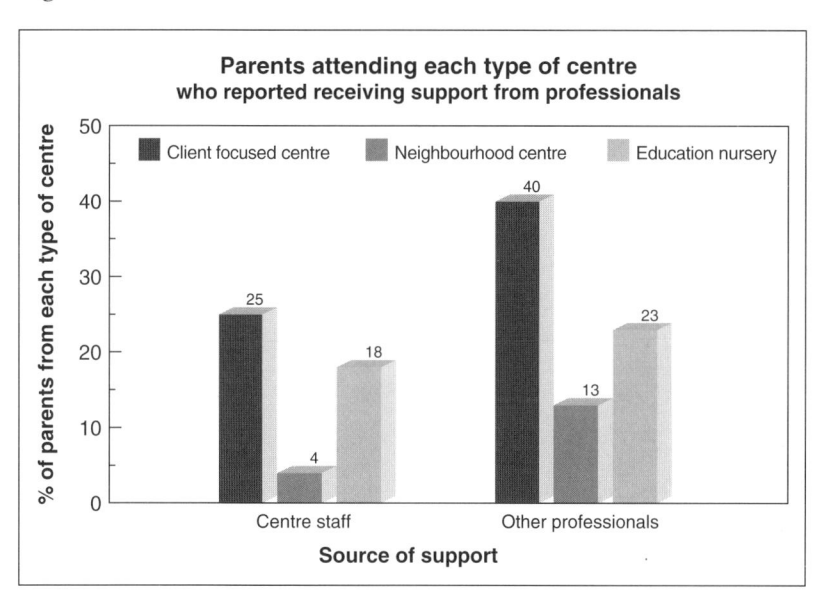

Parents attending each type of centre who reported receiving support from professionals

Source of support	Client focused centre	Neighbourhood centre	Education nursery
Centre staff	25	4	18
Other professionals	40	13	23

(% of parents from each type of centre)

Parents with critically high stress scores had significantly more need for advice, emotional support and opportunities to socialise. Around two thirds of parents with health problems, compared to a third without, had significantly more conflict in their relationships, greater need for help with child care, emotional and practical support. The families experiencing the greatest difficulties coping had fewer relatives available to support them and had the greatest need for support of various kinds. They were most likely to depend on professionals to meet these needs. Those who attended neighbourhood centres may have had the strongest informal support systems, reducing reliance on professionals

Social isolation

Almost one in four of the families who used client focused centres went nowhere other than the centre on most days. This contrasts with one in ten of those who went to nurseries and neighbourhood centres. There were also significant differences between the 70% of parents who already knew other parents when their children started nursery in comparison to around 30%

of those attending a family centre. Although the age differences of the children may have played a part there remains further indication of the relative isolation of families using client focused centres from other sources of support.

Perceptions of centre function and family support

Parents' expectations of centre support were assessed by asking them whether or not they saw it as one of the main purposes of their centre. Over half of the parents saw the purpose as related exclusively to children's development while just under a third (32.9%) viewed the purpose of the centre as providing social support as well. One of the parents commented:

> *It helps stressed parents and benefits the children at the same time. It lets parents know that they are not on their own. Quite a few single parents use the centre and it is somewhere for them to go. I felt quite alone before. In the house and nowhere to go.*

When asked what the main differences were between nursery and the two models of family centre, around half were uncertain. The feature that was used to distinguish centres most frequently (22 cases) was whether or not the child could be left without the parent i.e. whether day care and education was available. Parental involvement and family support were mentioned by nine parents:

- *You can get help here. You can go to the staff with any problems*
- *...parents are more involved and welcomed into the playroom.*

A very small number (5), differentiated nurseries from family centres using educational terms.

- *...children are taught their colours.*
- *It is more of a teaching place.*

Despite the disparities in perceptions of the functions of nurseries and family centres, the majority of parents (83.1%) who responded expressed the view that all types of early years centres should provide support. Moreover they wanted this to be aimed at both parents and not just the mother (88%):

- *There should be support for parents with difficulties in the family, just someone to talk to, maybe a chance to talk to other parents about problems.*
- *...to help working parents with childcare, to give advice on stages of development and so on. People forget that there are men who need help too. Fathers should be able to get more involved.*

Different families, different needs?
Early years provision and social support

All the centres in the study worked conscientiously to provide high quality services within a community which experienced considerable disadvantage. The provision was highly valued by the families who used it, most of whom were relatively poor and under various kinds of stress. Even within a community in which there might be thought to be much similarity between families and their needs, there were distinctive differences between those who used different types of provision. The segregation of children using different forms of provision was striking. The poorest, most socially isolated families, who were often lone parents, had the weakest informal support networks with few relatives available to support them. Many experienced conflict in their inter-personal relationships. They frequently had children with developmental delay. They needed advice and information, someone in whom they could confide, opportunities to meet others and to have help with babysitting. The majority of these families attended client-focused family centres which did provide the kind of formal supports that were essential to them.

In the Region in which these centres were based, admissions were operated on a combination of an open and closed referral system. This helped to reduce stigma yet clearly operated in such a way that families with the greatest needs were obtaining the majority of the places. The neighbourhood family centres depended on building up informal support networks amongst parents rather than create dependence on professionals to achieve their family support goals. The needs of the parents who attended these centres were more mixed as a whole but included some very vulnerable families who might have been reluctant to use traditional types of services and clearly benefited from the support they received. The low levels of stress are worth further investigation. The families who attended the nurseries were more materially advantaged yet they also showed high levels of stress and a quarter had children with developmental delay. Professional support was an important feature of their lives although the nurseries did not view this as one of their responsibilities. It will be important to examine the differences in outcomes that take place over the course of the subsequent year.

Parents use early years provision for many different reasons but the service they receive appears to reflect the primary function and admission system of the centre rather than an informed choice on the part of parents. This is supported by parents' apparent lack of understanding of the differences between centres. While it may be argued by providers that the parents' needs varied and as a consequence there was a match made with the resources used, this cannot detract from the overall effect of providing one set of young children with a different experience of early years provision from another, primarily on the basis of family income. Without a comprehensive infrastructure which makes early years provision widely available, parents have to make complex, individualised arrangements if they wish to work or provide their children with opportunities to have stimulating learning opportunities with their peers. Access depends on the parents' abilities to pay for, negotiate and organise a place in an early years centre as well as their access to relatives and friends who are able to offer supplementary child care when the hours of the provision do not match the needs of parents. Some parents lack the personal, material or social resources this requires. These are the families most likely to be found using family centres rather than other types of early years provision.

The centre models in the study could each be viewed as targeting intervention at different levels to achieve the same goal of enhancing child development The nurseries concentrated on the individual child's development within the nursery, the client-focused centre was also concerned with the child within the centre and home-centre links. The neighbourhood centre focused on parents, the relationships within and between young families within the context of the local community. It could be argued that the differences in approach and services offered reflected the professional training and experience of staff and the wider goals of the funding agencies as much as diversity of family needs. This creates confusion for parents and allows professional interests to predominate and segregation to be justified.

Poverty and social integration

It has been argued that poverty is one of the most important factors underlying the stresses experienced by many families at risk from child abuse and neglect. This is compounded by a lack of social support (Deccio et al.,1994). The extent of 'social integration' within the neighbourhood has also been viewed as a significant risk factor. Social integration can be seen as comprising three main components in which social support within the neighbourhood was one and the other two involved the parent's sense of power and their relations to the world of work. As a concept it goes beyond the interpersonal dimension of social support to address structural elements such as unemployment and its impact on the individual as well as the neighbourhood. Deccio et al. argued that:

> *Public and private child welfare agencies should seek to create employment opportunities for unemployed adults in low income families as well as encouraging participation in community groups and activities.* (p.136.)

Work has been shown not only to provide financial and material benefits, but also can give a sense of achievement and purpose. It creates opportunities to develop social relationships and enhance self-esteem (Locke and Taylor, 1991). Only the client-focused centres aimed to provide day care for working parents and operated a full day service which could most easily respond flexibly to parents in work and yet the percentage of working parents was lower than in the other centres although users were equally well and better qualified. Early years provision which enables women to work as well as meeting the developmental needs of the child have been given lower priority than the development of therapeutic, community development and educational approaches in the public sector, yet the gains which could be achieved by the disadvantaged groups who use local authority provision are often those which welfare agencies seek to achieve.

Early years provision and social integration

The 1995 Children Act review was the last one prior to local government reorganisation in 1996. It must be used positively to minimise undermining the progress which has been made by authorities that have worked hard in recent years to improve co-ordination and introduce developments in this field. The continuing absence of central government funding, direction and mandate to provide preschool services, allows the conflicting perspectives embodied by local authority services to be perpetuated i.e. rationing and targeting on the one hand and universalism and equal opportunities on the other. Many of them are in an impossible position, trying as they do, to satisfy the challenges made from both directions.

Children and families lose out while the debate continues, fuelled by the shortage of provision. The mixed economy solution reinforces class divisions and the segregation of families. It is important that development is not merely an extension of the existing divisiveness which persists in this field, much of it based on professional interests. The clear view, expressed by the majority of parents in this study, that family support should be an integral part of all early years services is important. Similarly, the changing needs of families, for men to become more actively involved in the care of their children and women to work, must shape the future of early years services as they have such a powerful potential to enhance social integration and improve the quality of life of so many. It is important that an informed public debate directs central and local government as they respond to the high unmet needs for early years services.

References

Abidin, R. B. (1990) *Parenting Stress Manual.* Charlottesville: Paediatric Psychology Press.

Barnett, W. S (1993) Benefit-cost analysis of preschool education: findings from a 25 year follow-up. *American Journal of Orthopsychiatry.* 63, 4, 500–508.

Bellman, M. and Cash, J. (1987) *The Schedule of Growing Skills in Practice.* London: NFER–Nelson.

Belsky, J. (1984) The determinants of parenting: A processes model. *Child Development,* 55, 83–96.

Bronfenbrenner, U. (1979) *The Ecology of Human Development.* Cambridge: Harvard University Press.

Canaan, C. (1990) Supporting the family? An assessment of family centres. In *Social Policy Review 1989–1990.* (eds. N. Manning and C. Ungerson). London: Longman.

Canaan, C. (1992) *Changing Families; Changing Welfare.* Hemel Hempstead: Harvester Wheatsheaf.

Central Statistical Office (1993) *Social Trends, 23.* London: HMSO.

Chan, Yuk Chung (1994) Parenting stress and social support of mothers who physically abuse their children in Hong Kong. *Child Abuse and Neglect.* 18, 3, 261–269.

Cochran, M., Larner, M., Riley, D., Gunnarsson, L. and Henderson, C.R.(1990) *Extending Families: The Social Networks of Parents and Their Children.* Cambridge: Cambridge University Press.

Cohen, B. (1990) *Caring for Children. The 1990 Report.* Edinburgh: Family Policies Studies Centre and Scottish Child and Family Alliance.

Cohen, S. and Syme, S. L. eds. (1985) *Social Support and Health.* Orlando: Academic Press.

Culbertson, J. L. and Schellenbach, C. J. (1992) Prevention of maltreatment in infants and young children. In *Prevention of Child Maltreatment: Developmental and Ecological Perspectives.* D. Willis, E. W. Holden and M.Rosenberg (eds). New York: Wiley and Sons.

Deccio, G., Horner, W. C. and Wilson, D. (1994) High-risk neighbourhoods and high-risk families: Replication research related to the human ecology of child maltreatment. *Journal of Social Service Research.*18, 3/4, 123–137.

Dunst, C., Trivette, C. and Deal, A. (1988) *Enabling and Empowering Families: Principles and Guidelines for Practice.* Cambridge, MA: Brookline Books.

Family Policy Studies Centre (1993) Work and the Family. *Family Policy Bulletin,* December 1993.

Garbarino, J., and Sherman, D.(1980) High-risk neighbourhoods and high-risk families: The human ecology of child maltreatment. *Child Development,* 51, 1,188–198.

Gaudin, J., Polansky, N., Kilpatrick, A., and Shilton, P. (1993) Loneliness, depression, stress and social supports in neglectful families. *American Journal of Orthopsychiatry.* 63, 4, 597–604.

Gibbons, J., Thorpe, S. and Wilkinson, P. (1990) *Family Support and Prevention Studies in Local Areas.* London: HMSO.

Goldberg, D. (1978) *The General Health Questionnaire.* London: NFER–Nelson.

Goldschmied, E. and Jackson, S.(1994) *People Under Three; Young Children in Day Care.* London; Routledge.

Harman, D. and Brim, O.G. (1980) *Learning to be Parents; Principles, Programs and Methods.* Beverley Hills: Sage.

Hill, M.(1989) The role of social networks in the care of young children. *Children and Society.* 3, 195–211.

Holman, B. (1988) *Putting Families First: Prevention and Child Care.* London: Macmillan.

Kirk, R. (1990) Family centres for the '90s, *Scottish Child,* August – September, 10–11.

Kirk, R. (1994) Working the process through: Tayside Region. In *The Children Act Review: A Scottish Experience*. (ed. Carolyn Martin) Edinburgh: HMSO.

Krahn, G. (1993) Conceptualizing social support in families of children with special health needs, *Family Process*, 32, 235–248.

Locke, E. A. and Taylor, M. S. (1991) Stress, coping and the meaning of work. In A. Monat and R. S. Lazarus (eds.) *Stress and Coping*. New York: Columbia University Press.

Martyn, C. (ed.) (1994) *The Children Act Review: A Scottish Experience*. Edinburgh: HMSO.

McGurk, H., Caplan, M., Hennessy, E. and Moss, P. (1993) Controversy, theory and social context in contemporary day care research, *Journal of Child Psychology and Psychiatry*, 34, 1, 3–23.

Moos, R. H. (ed.) (1986) *Coping with Life Crisis: An Integrated Approach*. New York: Plenum Press.

Pennycook, J. (1991) *Scottish Family Centre Directory*. Scottish Association of Family Centres.

Scottish Child and Family Alliance (1992) *Scotland's Families Today*. Edinburgh: SCAFA, HMSO.

Scarr, S. and Eisenberg, M.(1993) 'Child care research; Issues, perspectives, and results' *Annual Review of Psychology*, 44, 613–44.

Scottish Office: Social Work Services Group (1993). *Scotland's Children; Proposals for Child Care Policy and Law*. Edinburgh: HMSO.

Weiss, H. B. and Jacobs, F.H. (eds) (1988) *Evaluating Family Programs*. New York: Aldine de Gruyter.

Williams, F. (1989) *Social Policy: A Critical Introduction*. Cambridge & Oxford: Polity Press and Basil Blackwell.

8

SOCIAL WORK SERVICES FOR YOUNG PEOPLE

Malcolm Hill, John Triseliotis and Moira Borland

Young people, parents and social work

WHEREAS preceding chapters have been concerned with younger children, this one focuses on services for young people and their families. It is based on a three year research study funded by the Department of Health which examined the impact of measures of supervision and care in five local authorities in England and Scotland. Our study was concerned with those young people whose behaviour or situation was sufficiently troubling to bring them to the attention of Social Services or Social Work Departments.

It is a common belief amongst adults that most if not all adolescents are difficult, moody, wayward and volatile. Young people themselves are more inclined to feel put upon by adults with unrealistic and unreasonable expectations. In fact this stereotype of mutual suspicion, disrespect and recrimination is misleading. Although minor disagreements are common, most adolescents get on well with their families and other adults. The majority of parents effect a gradual transfer of autonomy, rights and responsibilities to their teenage offspring within a context of continuing support and modified parental authority (Coleman and Hendry, 1990; Triseliotis et al., 1993).

Of course there are exceptions, as headlines about joyriders, truants, young burglars and even child murderers remind us. Furthermore the transition to adulthood is not easy at a time of high youth unemployment, limited income for young adults out of work, ubiquitous media encouragement to consumption and strong but fragmented peer subcultures. When difficulties arise in the teen years, there is usually a combination of influences of 3 main kinds:

- responses by the young person and significant others in their lives to the developmental tasks and status ambiguity of *adolescence as a life phase*
- *particular biographical factors and relationships* of the individual and family
- wider *social and economic circumstances*, in particular those affecting educational and employment prospects.

When imbalances have arisen amongst the needs, expectations, behaviour and resources of young people and significant adults in their lives, it is the task of professionals to help bring these into line with each other by means of adjustments on one or both sides. In recent years there have been a number of competing nostrums to guide social service responses to young people with difficulties. Each has its merits, but they have sometimes been applied too generally. For example, with regard to placements away from home, residential care has been portrayed in certain quarters as invariably an undesirable last resort, whilst others assert that it can be a positive choice. Some people argue that fostering is largely irrelevant for placing adolescents, yet others claim that even the most demanding young person can be fostered.

A major influence on policy and practice has been the principle of diversion from statutory measures or formal care whenever possible. Diversion may be largely passive (gatekeeping, cautioning) or more active (e.g. intermediate treatment, alternatives to custody), in which case it overlaps with prevention. Diversionary ideas have been applied successfully in relation to young offenders and helped reduce the numbers of young people living apart from their families (Pitts, 1988). However there are dangers when the principle is applied in an oversimplified manner (Kearney and Mapstone, 1992). Both legislation and practice recognise that some parents cannot provide adequate controls without formal external support, whilst substitute care can be a positive choice to meet the needs and/or wishes of some young people.

The study

Responses to young people and their families thus encompass a spectrum of measures ranging from minimal intervention via support at home to care placements and secure accommodation. In our study, we examined the impact on young people and their families of the full range of services provided in five different local authorities – three in England and two in Scotland (Triseliotis et al., 1994). A sample was recruited of 116 young people, aged 13–17, who were experiencing the start of a new form of social services intervention or a significant change in care or supervision arrangements.

The study was planned on a longitudinal basis in order to ascertain progress following intervention and compare this with expectations. The young person, social worker and parents in every case were each interviewed twice approximately one year apart, except when a potential respondent was unavailable or unwilling to be seen. In the interviews, problems, services and current circumstances were discussed in depth. On both occasions, information was gathered on the seven dimensions identified as significant by the DoH Assessing Outcomes Project (Parker et al., 1991):

- health
- education
- behaviour
- social and family relationships
- self-care
- identity
- self presentation.

The measures included standardised Rutter and Coopersmith scales, which assess psychosocial development and self-esteem respectively (Rutter et al., 1970; Coopersmith, 1990).

In the remainder of this chapter, we summarise very briefly the circumstances at referral and then concentrate on:

- our findings concerning the types of services deployed
- the evidence gathered about the effectiveness of those services.

Problems and expectations

Offending, family conflict and school related problems were the dominant issues leading to referral to social services and the three were closely interrelated. Relationship difficulties between parents and young people caused much unhappiness and bad feeling. The older the young person the more likely that conflict at home dominated the issues. Separation and family reconstitution were at the heart of many conflicts. These interpersonal problems were usually accompanied by low achievement at school and very few of those who left school were in work.

Parents' attempts to obtain help from the social work services early on had mixed receptions, so that many thought intervention had come too late. With most of the spotlight being on child protection involving younger children, preventive work with young people was not usually seen as a priority by the agencies.

When it came to the participants' initial expectations of intervention, important differences emerged. Social workers tended to set long term goals, which included personal development. They often aimed to help young people develop confidence and skills to cope with life challenges. In contrast, young people and parents were inclined to focus on immediate and tangible action to meet their practical needs or modify what they saw as unacceptable behaviours or attitudes on the part of the other. The lack of agreement about expectations suggests a low level of explicit sharing in problem definition and planning, in spite of the recent emphasis on closer participation and joint planning between social workers and service users. As a result, some young people and parents disapproved of what social workers did partly because they did not understand the reasons and purposes.

Services provided

Within our sample of 116 young people, 36 received care services while living away from home all year, 44 experienced only supervision at home and 36 combined the two. Across the five authorities social workers brought into play a wide *range of services,* including some provided by other agencies. The most common were:

> ***Away from home*** *– residential units; residential schools; foster care; preparation for independence units and supported accommodation.*
>
> ***Home or away*** *– outreach or befriending by residential carers or volunteers; day places in residential schools; group work; psychological and psychiatric services; special education classes or unit; home tuition.*

However in no agency was the full range routinely available. There was nearly always a delay between a request for residential education or foster care and its actual provision. Depending on agency policy and local resources, group work, befriending, outreach and foster care were each widely used in some areas, but rarely or not at all in others. Consequently allocation of services resulted as much from local provision and custom as from young people's needs or preferences.

By the follow-up stage of the study, 26 young people were or had been living 'independently' of their primary family, but space does not permit detailed attention here to this subsample. In broad terms their needs and experiences repeated those identified previously (Stein & Carey, 1986; Garnett, 1992). Most felt lonely and unsupported, many encountered financial, housing and relationship difficulties.

Residential care

The two main forms of institutional care provided were residential units (mainly for reception/assessment or multi-purpose) and residential schools. Units ranged in size from six to twenty residents. Commonly residential placements of all types were regarded as a last resort (cf. Packman et al., 1986), so that admissions were arranged hurriedly and with little choice as regards suitability.

Placements in residential schools were the most durable, usually lasting about a year or more, whereas many of the placements in residential units lasted a matter of weeks or months. There was therefore little stability of living companions. The duration of placements often bore little relationship to the original plan. For example only a quarter each of the residential unit and foster care placements which had been expected to last a year actually did so, compared with 60% of the residential school placements. Besides having a larger and steadier population, residential schools had more organised programmes.

Foster care

The relevance of foster care to teenagers remains contested (Hazel, 1990; Cliffe with Berridge, 1991) and this was apparent in the diversity of provision. One of the study agencies had very few foster places available, so that fostering was seldom considered. By contrast, another had a specialist foster scheme solely for teenagers and also a remand fostering scheme. Both projects operated with written contracts and additional pay compared with regular fostering. A third agency had dismantled its specialist schemes and introduced higher rates of pay for all foster carers, so that young people were placed within the general fostering system. Even so, in all agencies there was normally a delay of at least several months between the request for placement and an opening. Nevertheless, foster care was an important resource for this age group, representing roughly one third of all the placements experienced by the sample:

	Res. Care	Foster Care
No. of young people placed during year	55	27
No. of placements in total	78	37

Befriending and outreach

These are forms of individualised support to young people at home, arranged to supplement the social worker's own contribution. Befriending refers to contacts by volunteers; outreach is done by staff operating from a base in residential care.

Apart from one team which made regular use of outreach workers based in its area, the availability and take-up of befriending seemed idiosyncratic. In all, just over one sixth of the sample had been offered either befriending or outreach. It was arranged in three kinds of circumstance:
- for males on home supervision, who were usually taken out to engage in recreational activities (we did not encounter comparable provision for females)
- for young people in care, partly to relieve pressures on staff/carers
- for young adults living on their own (though only a few in this position were offered befriending).

Group work

Just over two fifths of the young people said they had been offered group work during the year, of whom three quarters had actually attended. There were three main types of group, nearly all run by social service or youth justice workers:

- diversionary activity groups
- groups focusing on cognitive and behavioural change in relation to offending or addictions
- 'in care' or 'leaving care' discussion groups

The first two were mainly concerned with behaviour management and prevention, the last with promoting awareness and self-confidence (Bottoms et al., 1990).

Although 'in care' groups were attended equally by girls and boys, nearly all of those on supervision who were offered a group were boys. Group work was also used more often for younger rather than older adolescents, apart from specialist projects focusing on offending or addictions. One agency's policy was that group work should be the main form of intervention for young people in the community, so that attendance rates there were much higher than elsewhere (four fifths offered).

Referral to other agencies

The study was primarily concerned with specialist provision over which Social Services/Work Departments had direct control. Nevertheless, it was evident that the difficulties faced by many young people were affected by other agencies. Collaboration with other agencies differed markedly, depending on the legislative and local context. For instance, an English Authority co-operated closely with the probation service and police, as well as several voluntary agencies, whereas in two Scottish authorities strongest ties were with education departments, both having joint liaison panels attached to all secondary schools. One of the key gaps in resources identified by social workers was in specialist day school provision. Ironically, some of the best day schooling for those with special needs was present in residential schools, but this was not necessarily accessible by young people still at home.

Nearly one third of the sample had been offered the chance to see a psychologist or psychiatrist, and one quarter had actually done so. Most of the contacts were quite brief, either because the purpose was assessment or else the young person stopped attending. Only a few were keen to have specialised therapy, e.g.

– *Because of my temper, it's really bad.*
– *I was cracking up.*

The social worker's direct work

Alongside all of these services was the direct work of the social workers themselves. Occasionally their role was confined to assessment, service provision and case management functions, but usually they also sought to offer other kinds of help such as individual counselling, family work, mediation and advocacy. In rather more than half the cases where the young person experienced only home supervision, the social worker's input was the sole service provided (25 out of 44).

Typically social workers met with young people once or twice a month, whether the young person was in care or at home. According to social workers, their discussions were largely problem-focused and task-centred, though nearly half said they talked about family relationships. Whilst social workers often set aims which included personal development, in actual face to face work they appeared much more practically oriented. Young people confirmed that there was mainly a concern with the here and now, with much attention to schooling. By contrast, health issues were hardly ever mentioned.

In half the cases, social workers saw parents just as often as the young person, but in a substantial minority of cases parents received considerably less time. Often contact was separate and in a third of cases there was no joint contact with both young person and parents at all during the year. Furthermore joint contact was frequently unplanned or occurred at a formal review meeting, so that a deliberate strategy of family work or mediation was not common.

Feedback and outcomes at the end of the year

On a range of indicators, the situations of most young people had improved by the end of the year. For the sample as a whole, the proportion who had a very high Rutter score (i.e. were very 'disturbed') nearly halved, falling from 63% to 36%. Many were thought by their social workers to have gained in self-esteem, although the Coopersmith ratings showed little change in the overall pattern for the sample. Two thirds of the young people said their situation was better at the end of the year than at the start and over four fifths reported being satisfied with the way things had turned out.

This is an encouraging picture given the severity of the problems at the outset. Nevertheless, it cannot be assumed that the improvements were largely or even partly as a result of the intervention. 'Natural recuperation', dying down of family crises, other life changes and the optimism and resilience of many young people may all have played a part. Therefore it is important to examine the detailed feedback given about the intervention and to see which ones were associated with greater or less success. Besides the 'objective' measures referred to earlier like the Rutter scale and the Coopersmith Self-Esteem Inventory, social workers, young people and parents were asked about the benefits or disadvantages associated with each type of intervention, how helpful it had been and its impact on the original problems. In the summary of feedback and outcomes that follows, we separate for the sake of clarity those who received services at home from those who received a service away from home, but it must be remembered that nearly one third of the sample experienced both supervision and care.

Supervision at home

In spite of the long tradition of social work supervision of children and young people, there has been a dearth of studies to highlight the purpose, content/process and outcome of supervision. Parsloe's (1976) comment that supervision 'can mean anything or nothing' is as true now as it was almost 20 years ago when she first made it. When the purpose of supervision is examined in the social work literature, it is frequently in relation to compulsory measures mainly for adults supervised by probation officers, with the debate focusing mostly on how far it is desirable or feasible to combine 'care and control' (Raynor, 1985; Singer, 1989).

The majority of young people passively accepted supervision as a reasonable price to pay for their behaviour or for not 'being sent away'. Some even liked it and only about a fifth said that they hated it.

Whichever way the data were looked at, they showed that within the one year follow up period, about half the young people seemed to obtain some benefit from supervision, with the original problem disappearing or subsiding. A major feature of the analysis was the low level of agreement among the three 'actors' as to who exactly were the young people who benefited a lot, a little or none at all. Sometimes opposite views were held by social workers and young people about the outcome of intervention. Whilst it would be surprising to find a total consensus, it seems that rarely had there been a sharing of evaluations to reach a common conclusion. Young people who liked supervision mostly also saw it as beneficial. The opposite was true for those who were definite that they did not like supervision.

Social workers described the benefits from supervision for the young person as including:
- the reduction of offending
- preventing admission to care
- building up self-confidence and self-respect
- having someone to support the young person, be listened to and ensure that practical needs such as accommodation and food are ensured.

When they perceived little benefit, social workers attributed this to the young person's lack of motivation, to being difficult to engage with and to the family situation being resistant to change. There was little or no reference to resources or wider social factors as influencing the outcome.

Young people who perceived supervision as helpful saw it as improving their behaviour, as exercising a restraining influence on their behaviour, keeping them out of care, providing emotional or practical support or directing them to useful diversionary activities. Where young people made a resolve to stop offending, they achieved a fair amount of success. Several young people said they had been assisted to stop or reduce offending by social workers challenging them about their behaviour. However, this only happened when there was a good relationship between the two. Otherwise challenges were resented as interference or nagging and so were counter-productive. This supports the contention that control is helpful provided that it occurs within a caring relationship.

Unlike social workers only a few young people acknowledged developmental gains. This occurred when social workers had succeeded in encouraging the young person to take a longer term and more insightful view of their situation. When expectations remained divergent, then both parties were likely to feel frustrated by lack of progress.

Young people agreed with the social workers on the first two reasons for the absence of benefits from supervision, that is their lack of motivation and difficulty to engage with the social worker, but for the third they referred to the actions or inaction of social workers. They spoke of social workers being unreliable, not listening, not keeping promises or as being nosy.

Parents saw the benefits of supervision in behavioural terms such as the reduction of offending and of improved behaviour at home. In their view a major stumbling block leading to lack of progress was the absence of social work 'know-how' or suitable resources. One of the social work roles that received considerable approval by parents was the exercise of firmness. They also valued arrangements for the young person to attend clubs, groups and out-reach type activities. Social workers were not always aware of the importance parents attached to these types of social work action. Sometimes a mismatch of perception arose, because parents wanted 'firmness' and social workers realised they could not begin to exercise restraint until a good relationship had been built up. However, they had not explained this strategy to the parents, who simply concluded that the worker was being too soft.

For those young people who were supervised at home (and indeed for those in care) the quality of the personal *relationship with the social worker* was often vital. Very few reported getting on badly with their social worker, but there was a definite association between getting on *very well* and benefiting from supervision, in the eyes of both the adolescents and their parents. Young people reported the following characteristics as what they liked about social workers:

- being reliable and interested

- being straight and taking time
- understanding and listening
- continuity
- keeping confidences
- being informal and attending to practical concerns.

These correspond with the classic features of good counselling such as empathy and respect, together with reliability and practical action. In these regards, they wanted what adult consumers of social work services have been found to value (Rees and Wallace, 1982). Here are typical positive comments:

– *The social worker stopped me getting put away for not going to school. She is really interested in me. She makes you want to be good.*

– *You could talk away to him what you want and he would listen to you. He makes you feel comfortable. He made me feel better about myself.*

The main complaints made by young people about social workers were the reverse of these qualities, namely unreliability, inaccessibility, lack of interest, lecturing the young person, being pushy and being too formal. Some young people also felt that the social services wanted to get rid of them at 16:

– *I haven't seen a social worker since I last saw you.*
– *I felt they should accept their responsibility and not try to get rid of me.*

A minority saw supervision as intrusive – 'checking on you', 'showing you up at school' or 'taking up your time'.

Parents' views about social workers closely paralleled those of the young people. They also liked social workers who were available, willing to help, friendly, easy to talk to and listening. One parent summed it up as follows:

She lets me talk, lets me put my ideas, work out where to go next and what to do.

Within the period of twelve months, just over a fifth of those who started on supervision had either gone into care or custody. The rest of the young people were about equally split between those who were still continuing on supervision and those who had finished. The most common reasons quoted by social workers as dangers for a young person going into care or custody were offending behaviour and drugs, followed by conflict at home or a combination of these two factors.

Care programmes away from home

Taken together, our measures of progress and participants' views revealed very different pictures of the success of the three main forms of placement:

- **residential schools** – very positive outcomes
- **residential units** – more ambivalent and mixed outcomes
- **foster care** – tended to be either very successful or disappointing.

Residential units and schools

In general, young people were very positive about residential care staff, but some were less so about the placement in general. Shortly after admission to residential care, most youngsters described themselves as 'accepting' the situation, with a quarter feeling 'pleased to be there' and a few ' unhappy'. Most liked the general physical environment, though a number commented adversely on the lack of privacy (cf. Gardner, 1989). A high value was placed on adult companionship and understanding. They liked staff who were friendly, informal and who listened with respect to their viewpoints. Whilst carers who were young and had similar interests to themselves were popular, the more discerning recognised that deeper qualities were desirable too. One youngster said:

> *We got on well, liked the same music, but she seemed too much like a friend to discuss serious or personal things.*

The chief criticisms about residential establishments were that some were too far from home and that certain other residents were difficult to get on with. Bullying is a major concern of young people in residential care (Buchanan et al., 1993) and in our sample one in six said they had been bullied or ill-treated. Certain rules, particularly about home leave and times for getting in at night, were resented in both units and schools.

Nearly all the young people who had attended residential schools spoke positively about them. They told us proudly that they were now making progress after long periods of failure. They liked the individual attention, non-competitive atmosphere and the wide range of activities including crafts and workshops. Approving comments included:

– *People don't laugh at you.*
– *Teachers explain things.*
– *Everyone is in the same boat.*
– *Classes are small.*

'Access' issues differed from those affecting younger children (Millham et al., 1986; Hess and Proch, 1988). Contact with family was rarely problematic. Whereas young children normally rely on parents to visit them, adolescents can go home themselves, which nearly all were allowed to do as frequently as they wanted. On the other hand, almost half would have preferred to see their friends more often than they were permitted.

Parents too mostly had good relationships with residential staff and over 80% said they got on well. The main qualities they welcomed were friendliness and helpfulness towards themselves and concern for the young person combined with firm controls. When they were critical, this was usually as a result of what they saw as lax discipline. For example:

- *He never learns discipline there. He escapes punishment.*
- *He does what he likes. We told the staff they did not know their jobs.*

These criticisms mostly applied to residential units and only one parent expressed dissatisfaction with a residential school. Parents' expectations were fulfilled with respect to 85% of residential school placements, but only 42% of residential unit placements. In several instances parents of school non-attenders were very thankful that their children were at last receiving some education at residential school.

At the end of the year, field social workers stated that they were satisfied or very satisfied with all the residential school placements and two thirds of the residential unit placements. In both types of establishment, relationships with staff were seen as crucial. Social workers referred to the support, attention and advice given. Also important was 'space' or 'respite' away from home to take stock or discontinue unhelpful patterns of behaviour or interaction. Temporary separation might be sufficient to allow feelings over a dispute with parents to die down and modified rules to be negotiated. In other instances it was clear that longer term 'shared care' was needed. As one young woman herself stated:

- *We can get on fine, but if we're in the same house too long, then things don't work out.*

To some extent, social workers agreed with parents about care and control issues. With respect to one fifth of the residential unit places, they thought there was insufficient control, but they were nearly always content with the quality of care, security and discipline provided in residential schools.

Turning to our measures of progress, we found that those young people who had spent some or part of the year in a residential school included a higher proportion whose self-esteem improved during the year than the sample as a whole (based on both Coopersmith forms and social workers' assessments). Several of the schools placed great emphasis on acceptance and finding imaginative ways of making young people feel good about themselves.

Foster placements
Feedback about foster placements was complex. When placements had been completed during the course of the year, far more were thought to have ended prematurely than was the case for residential placements. On the other hand, nearly all continuing placements were regarded very positively.

Even when placements were thought not to have lasted as long as planned or needed, usually some gains from placement were acknowledged and it was rare for the young person to have got on poorly with all members of the foster family.

What young people liked about foster care included close trust, feelings of being cared for and involvement in family activities. Relative freedom compared with the parental home or residential care was also valued. Several said that fostering had helped improve their behaviour, school work or consideration for others. Resentments about foster care mostly centred on what young people saw as attempts to restrict their autonomy or intrude on their self-sufficiency. These seemed to reflect deep-seated attachment patterns, as Downes (1992) has suggested. Young adults used to detachment found it hard to fulfil expectations of close parental involvement in their lives. Problems resulted from a mismatch of expectations and superficiality in the agreements made at the start of placements, which is perhaps not surprising since some foster carers had no special training.

Overall outcomes

We devised a summary outcome measure based on a combination of Rutter scores, changes in self-esteem and participants' views of the intervention, progress over the year and future prospects. Interestingly, all of the 9 cases which were most 'successful' *and* had made most progress according to this combination of evidence involved young people who had been in care. Six were still in care and three had returned home. It is perhaps to be expected that the major environmental change involved in being in care should have more impact than supervision at home, but nevertheless this finding counters the common presumption that removal from home is a failure.

The summary measure could not be linked in a straightforward way to placement type, since many youngsters had experienced more than one, whilst the duration of care also varied greatly. However, well over half of those living in residential units at the end of the year were classified as 'not successful', compared with only one in ten in residential schools. This was partly because young people with unsuccessful foster placements or home supervision were likely to be admitted to a residential unit, as Berridge (1985) found.

Summary and implications of the study

The overall findings point to the need for greater openness and sharing at all stages, from the definition of the problem to the setting of expectations and the assessment of outcomes. As young people and parents mainly focus on short term goals, there is a need for regular feedback and review sessions to help re-define the problem and readjust goals where necessary. In addition, explanations should be given of social workers' methods and longer term strategies.

The range of services

The study revealed an impressive spectrum of services across the five agencies. Moreover in a number of instances these were helpfully combined, e.g. group work with residential care or supervision, family work with residential schooling. However, no individual agency had the full range routinely available. Most services were provided in some areas but not others. Even when a facility was available there was often a considerable delay in obtaining a place, as was typically true for both foster care and residential schools. The one service which could be relied on to be provided quickly was residential care, although not always of the right type or in the right location. If the most appropriate choices are to be made in the interests of young people, then more comprehensive services need to be available. In particular, foster care, group work and befriending should be among the options in all areas not just some. Each service can help some teenagers, yet our evidence suggests that some are not even considered when the social worker has little or no experience of them.

Supervision in the community

In spite of the fact that the resources deployed were found to be inconsistent and not always well co-ordinated, supervision in the community did achieve modest results. Almost four out of every five young people who were on supervision were still in the community twelve months later. Not all of those who stayed in the community, though, attributed the achievement to the benefits of supervision. Amongst the factors which appeared to have the most positive results were:

- supervision by an agency that has developed joint strategies with other departments, such as education;
- consistent and purposeful individual and family work which is based on a shared definition of problems and expectations;
- paying attention to both practical and social needs.

Work with young people who offend or exhibit behaviour difficulties went well when the social worker built up a positive relationship *and* was prepared to challenge young people to 'own' their behaviour and its consequences. Both group work and befriending were regarded as enjoyable elements in supervision, although less often were they seen as contributing to change. It appears necessary to make them more purposeful without losing their attractiveness for young people as enjoyable activities.

Residential and foster care

Many care placements were helpful, especially when combined with effective involvement of parents. For some individuals, substitute care can be helpful and ought to be considered not simply when all diversionary activity has failed. Often brief care is sufficient to enable crises and feelings to die down or to enable time-limited work to take place. For a small minority of young people, a more extensive and more expensive commitment may be needed, especially for those who at present are expected to leave care without an adequate support network.

Residential care was rarely a positive choice at the outset, but in fact often had positive outcomes. Usually young people's and parents' relationships with both residential and field social workers were good. Favourable feedback and outcomes were especially associated with residential schooling, although it must be remembered that our care sample mainly consisted of new entrants to the system. What appealed to young people and parents about the residential schools was partly the educational milieu, with less pressure and more individually tailored programmes. But also important were the organised programme and sense of purpose, together with the fact that care was shared with the family.

Foster care included instances of both the most successful and the least successful placements away from home. There were indications that careful preparation, contracting and matching are required if unsatisfactory endings are to be reduced.

Conclusions

This chapter has reported on a study of social work services provided for a sample of young people with many serious difficulties. Over the course of one year following social work intervention, the majority experienced an improvement in their situation. For the most part, they and their parents were positive about the assistance offered and there were many individual examples of effective practice. However a number of key services were unavailable in some areas or required a lengthy wait. There was a need for more integration and participation at both policy and operational levels. It is time that young people's needs and rights received the concerted and co-ordinated attention which has been given to child protection.

References

Berridge, D. (1985) *Children's Homes.* Oxford: Basil Blackwell.
Bottoms, A., Brown, P., McWilliams, B., McWilliams, W. and Nellis, M. (1990) *Intermediate Treatment and Juvenile Justice.* London: HMSO.

Buchanan, A., Wheal, A. and Coker, R. (1993) *Answering Back.* (Dolphin Project), University of Southampton: Department of Social Work Studies.

Cliffe, D. with Berridge, D. (1991) *Closing Children's Homes: An End to Residential Childcare?* London: National Children's Bureau.

Coleman, J. C. and Hendry, L. (1990) *The Nature of Adolescence.* London: Routledge, Chapman and Hall.

Coopersmith, S. (1990) *Self Esteem Inventories.* Palo Alto: Consulting Psychologists Press Inc.

Downes, C. (1992) *Separation Revisited.* Aldershot: Ashgate.

Gardner, R. (1989) 'Consumer Views' in B. Kahan (ed) *Child Care Research, Policy and Practice.* London: Hodder & Stoughton.

Garnett, L. (1992) *Leaving Care and After.* London: National Children's Bureau.

Hazel, N. (1990) 'The development of specialist foster care for adolescents: Policy and practice', in Galaway, B., Maglajlic, D., Hudson, J., Harmon, P. and McLagan, J. (eds.) *International Perspectives on Specialist Foster Family Care.* St Paul: Human Services Associates.

Hess, P. M. and Proch, K. O. (1988) *Contact : Managing visits to children looked after away from home.* London: BAAF.

Kearney, B. and Mapstone, E. (1992) *Report of the Inquiry into Child Care Policies in Fife.* Edinburgh: HMSO.

Millham, S., Bullock, R., Hosie, K. and Haak, M. (1986) *Lost in Care.* Aldershot: Gower.

Packman, J., Randall, J. and Jacques, N. (1986) *Who Needs Care?.* Oxford: Blackwell.

Parker, R., Ward, H., Jackson, S., Aldgate, J. and Wedge, P. (1991) *Assessing Outcomes in Child Care.* London: HMSO.

Parsloe, P. (1976) 'Social work and the justice model', *British Journal of Social Work,* 6:71–90.

Pitts, J. (1988) *The Politics of Juvenile Crime.* London: Sage.

Raynor, P. (1985) *Social Work, Justice and Control.* Oxford: Blackwell.

Rees, S. and Wallace, A. (1982) *Verdicts on Social Work.* London: Edward Arnold.

Rutter, M., Tizard, J. and Whitmore, K. (eds) (1970) *Education, Health and Behaviour.* London: Longman.

Singer, L. (1989) *Adult Probation and Juvenile Supervision.* Aldershot: Avebury.

Stein, M. and Carey, K. (1986) *Leaving Care.* Oxford: Blackwell.

Triseliotis, J., Borland, M. , Hill, M. and Lambert, L. (1993) 'The rights and responsibilities of young people in need or in trouble', *International Journal of Children's Rights.* 1: 315-330.

Triseliotis, J., Borland, M. , Hill, M. and Lambert, L. (1994) *Care Services for Teenagers.* Universities of Edinburgh and Glasgow: Final Report to the Department of Health.

9

SUPPORTING FAMILIES THROUGH INTER-AGENCY WORK: YOUTH STRATEGIES IN SCOTLAND

Andrew Kendrick

Introduction

IN this chapter, I will look at some of the developments in inter-agency work between social work, education, and other agencies which have taken place over recent years under the rubric of 'Youth Strategy'.[1] This work tends to focus on older children and I will not be looking at the wide range of multi-agency work with families of younger children (see Audit Commission, 1994; Kendrick, 1986).

In 1993, the Government issued the White Paper 'Scotland's Children' (Scottish Office, 1993), which set out recommendations for changes in child care law in the context of explicit principles incorporating the philosophy of the United Nations Convention on the Rights of the Child. Three of these principles are of particular relevance to the discussion of inter-agency collaboration.

The White Paper states that 'children have a right to express their views about any issues or decisions affecting or worrying them', and that due weight should be given to the views and concerns of children in reaching decisions. A second principle is that 'parents should normally be responsible for the upbringing and care of their children' but should be supported to fulfil their responsibilities to their children, and services to children and families should be delivered in partnership with parents. The last of the White Paper's eight principles is that 'any intervention in the life of a child, including the provision of supportive services, should be based on collaboration between all the relevant agencies'. Children are entitled to expect good education and health care and they have the right to expect that professionals from the different agencies will collaborate in a child-centred way by fulfilling their roles and by understanding and respecting others' contributions (Scottish Office, 1993. pp. 6–7).

These principles have been taken forward in the Children (Scotland) Bill (HMSO, 1994) where the provision for having regard to the views of children are set out in Clauses 5, 16 and 17. The Bill highlights the rights

---

[1] Research was funded by the Scottish Office Social Work Services Group and by Tayside Regional Council Social Work and Education Departments.

and responsibilities of parents in relation to their children, even when separated. There is a new general duty on local authorities to safeguard and promote the welfare of children and, so far as is consistent with that duty, to promote the upbringing of such children by their families. Clause 17 also places a duty on the local authority to have regard to the views of parents in making decisions about children. Local authorities are to be given a new duty to prepare and publish a plan for the provision of relevant services for children and in preparing this plan, the local authority shall consult a range of other agencies: Health Boards and Trusts; voluntary organisations; the Children's Panel; and the Reporter to the Children's Panel. Education Departments are not mentioned.

Social work and education

The need for the integration of child care services has long been recognised and stems from the disjointed and uneven way in which services have developed historically. The effect of this uneven development is that '... not only are resources wasted when services are uncoordinated, such lack of cohesion is harmful to children and their families' (Mapstone, 1983, p. 20). The seminal Kilbrandon Report (1964), besides recommending that the Children's Hearings system should be established in Scotland, also envisaged the establishment of a 'social education department' which would bring together both education and social work services for children. However, when social work services were reorganised in the late 1960s, it was considered preferable to create a unified service which brought together services for children, the mentally ill, the elderly and offenders (HMSO, 1966). Kilbrandon's 'social education department' was never set up and there has been a continued split in the provision of services for children between social work and education (Kendrick, forthcoming; Schaffer, 1992).

One result of the divide between social work and education has been a major frustration for the Children's Hearings system which has the power to require action by the former but not the latter. As Lockyer (1988) observed:

...many of the existing resources of importance for supporting children at home, in the hands of the local authority, are beyond their reach simply because they are 'owned' by local authority departments other than social work. When the duty is on the local authority to give effect to hearings' decision it seems odd that necessary local authority resources are beyond the reach of the hearing system. The inaccessibility of education resources are the major concern. (p. 32.)

This issue was addressed, at least in part, by the Scottish Child Care Law Review of the late 1980s which recommended that Children's Hearings should have access to the full range of local authority resources for children who reject normal schooling (Scottish Office, 1990, p. 29). These recommendations were accepted by the government in the White Paper 'Scotland's Children', which also stressed the importance of close co-operation between education and social work departments in the provision of services for children who do not attend school (Scottish Office, 1993, p. 36). Schaffer, however, suggested that the problem does not lie in the unwillingness of Education Departments to make existing resources available so much as 'in the stark reality that the full range of local authority resources for children who reject normal schooling is very limited' (Schaffer, 1992, p. 84).

Welton makes the important point that in the past:

...the idea that schools are an integral part of the welfare network for children and young people is not easily accepted either by teachers, or other professionals working with children and their families. (Welton, 1985, p. 62.)

The various professions have their own training, organisational and career structures which serve to promulgate separate perspectives and value bases. Nigel Bruce commented:

The student of the interface between social work and education in the 1980s resembles the anthropologist a hundred years ago, aiming to document and describe the confrontation between two widely different cultures. (Bruce, 1983, p. 153.)

He points out that, although the perspectives of social work and education may appear to overlap, researchers have often been struck more forcibly by the different perspectives of the two professions than by their similarities (Bruce, 1983, p. 161–162). Negative stereotyping of social workers by teachers, and vice versa, has occurred and this has been linked to respective training processes. One study found that negative stereotypes of the other profession were found with greater frequency among teaching and social work graduates than new entrants to courses (McMichael and Irvine, cited in Bruce, 1983, p. 163). McCullough (1991) stresses that inter-professional liaison and collaborative practice demands a very high level of knowledge and skills from the staff engaged in the process. The qualifying training of social workers and teachers, however, provides only limited opportunities to learn about the work of others and, indeed, as we saw above, the socialisation process of training may even reinforce mutual suspicion (McCullough, 1991).

Research has shown that children in care suffer from a number of educational disadvantages, even allowing for their social and environmental backgrounds. One important factor appears to be the low expectations held by social workers and care-givers of what children in care can achieve and the low priority they give to educational issues (Jackson, 1987; Jackson, 1989). From the educationalist's point of view, the needs of the disruptive individual have to be balanced against the needs of the class or school (Kearney, 1992). In research carried out by the author on 200 children in local authority care, one quarter of those of school age received into care had either been excluded or suspended before reception into care or were already in alternative educational provision: special day schools; attendance as day pupils at residential schools; alternative to learning projects; and intermediate treatment and college packages. Of the remainder, social workers reported that just under half of the children and young people in mainstream education had problems of non-attendance at school before they were received into care (Kendrick, forthcoming). The Fife Inquiry found a number of cases where children in the care of the Social Work Department did not receive any education for protracted periods (Kearney, 1992, p. 499).

Another important factor in the educational disadvantage of children and young people in care is the high level of disruption caused by movement between care placements which often involves a change of school (Berridge and Cleaver, 1987; Jackson, 1987). Berridge stressed that a disproportionately high number of the children in the children's homes studied had largely unsatisfactory educational experiences. He concluded that:

> *...the effects on a child's education had not always been fully considered when formulating social work plans and that continuity and coordination were often lacking.* (Berridge, 1985, p. 116).

In our study, almost three-fifths of the children experienced a change of school or alternative educational provision, either at admission to care or at a change of placement during the year of the study. One in ten had three or more changes of educational provision over the twelve months of the study (Kendrick, forthcoming).

These factors show that it is all the more vital that there is close co-operation and co-ordination of education and social work services and I now look at the strategies which local authority Social Work and Education Departments have, and are further developing, in order to improve such coordination and cooperation.

Youth strategies

Recent years have seen a number of initiatives in Scotland with the intention of creating more systematic co-ordination between social work, education and other agencies. Three local authorities have had youth strategies established for a number of years and several others have been developing strategies more recently (Gill and Pickles, 1989; Pickles, 1991).

The three long established youth strategies have varied in scope. The starting point of the strategies in Central Region and Lothian Region was related to keeping children out of residential education and developing a range of community-based resources to support children whose needs were not being met in mainstream education (Allan and Fearon, 1989; Maginnis, 1989). In both regions, the mechanism for 'systematic case co-ordination' was the School Liaison Group which consists of representatives from school guidance, educational psychology, the social work department, the school health service, and the community education service. This operates as a local, inter-agency group to intervene at an early stage to support young people experiencing difficulties. It is the intention that no young person will be excluded from secondary school or placed away from their community without assessment by the school liaison group and multi-disciplinary consideration of possible alternatives.

The youth strategies also involved the creation and development of jointly run alternative resources. For example, in Lothian Region specialist units have been established to provide a service for young people not able to remain whole-time in mainstream education. Young people attend the units for part of the time and their own school for part, with the aim of returning full-time to their own school as quickly as possible. The units also provide direct support to schools by helping to run small groups and individual programmes.

In Strathclyde Region, by contrast, the youth strategy was set in a broader policy framework which viewed young people in the wider social context of changing social relationships and deprivation. The youth strategy has been based on a 'community development' approach, establishing local 'Youth Development Teams'. These bring together agencies working with young people and community representatives to develop a range of opportunities and activities for young people in their area (Russell, 1989, p. 22).

An example of a more recent joint strategy is in Tayside Region. Here work began in October 1990 on an inter-departmental strategy to meet the needs of young people with special needs of a social or emotional nature. This has elements of both case-oriented and community development approaches. The strategy was to be:
- *comprehensive*, recognising the importance of family, voluntary organizations, churches and commercial interests in the lives of young people;
- *coordinated* at both regional and local level; and
- *inclusive*, addressing the needs of all young people up to the age of 19 years.

It was described as having three main goals: to maximise the effective use of human, physical and financial resources; to support, develop and involve agency staff; and to enable all young people whenever possible to be educated on their school site.

In October of 1992, the Strategy for Young People was launched. Six pilot areas held inaugural Tayside Region Youth Strategy Team (TRYST) meetings in the secondary schools bringing together a wide range of professional and community representatives to map out a local strategy. The issues raised were also wide-ranging:

- broad, social and economic issues such as youth unemployment, and young people's attitudes towards the family, community and society;
- the need for inter-agency co-operation and co-ordination;
- the need for resources, facilities and staff.

The local groups have developed the strategy in various ways. In some pilot areas, consultation with young people has been given the highest priority. For example, in one area an extensive survey exercise was carried out to find out what young people living locally wanted. In all pilot areas, an important contribution to the local strategies, led by Community Education, has been the setting up of Youth Enquiry Services. The local groups have also organized a number of activities and initiatives: a successful Fun Day for young people was organised; a local newsletter was set up; a project to support parents was formed in another area with input from community education, social work and the secondary school. One of the most successful aspects of the TRYST groups was the opportunity for different agencies to share perspectives, information and ideas.

So far I have concentrated on the community development aspect of the Strategy for Young People. Alongside this, the strategy developed a joint case conference and review structure. While this process did not run altogether smoothly, in early 1993 agreement was reached concerning a joint decision-making process to manage individual cases. This involves joint case conference at school and social work fieldwork level; joint management resource meetings; and joint directorate meetings to decide on special measures, extending exceptionally to residential care or education.

In addition to the decision-making process, Local Officer Groups were established consisting of the secondary school head-teacher, a primary school head-teacher representing 'cluster' schools, a senior manager in the social work department, a senior police officer and a representative of the community paediatric service. The Local Officer Group might additionally include representatives from community education and educational psychology. Its remit is to oversee the implementation of the corporate strategy at a local level. This is done by examining management information on children and young people in the secondary school catchment area, especially in relation to their movement through the five stage decision making process. Local Officer Groups also review the working links between agencies and actively consider ways of improving liaison and corporate working.

Inter-agency work is not un-problematic, however. Research involving interviews with social work staff across Scotland found that there was a great deal of variation in the relationships between social workers and secondary schools (Kendrick and Fraser, 1993). Even within one social work area team, relationships with different schools could be completely different. Some secondary schools were considered by social workers to try their hardest to accommodate the difficult and disruptive behaviour of young people, whereas other schools were thought to make little effort and to exclude pupils far too readily. It was often argued that the attitude of the head teacher was a principal factor in the success of relations between secondary schools and social work. Even where joint youth strategies were in operation, it was felt that coordination was unlikely to be effective if the head teacher was not supportive. Dryfoos (1993), in her review of school-based health and social services in the USA, comments on the key role of the school principal:

> *As the primary gatekeeper, the principal facilitates access to students, promotes good working relationships between the school staff and the program staff, and makes sure the building is safe and clean. If the principal does not cooperate, the program will not work.* (Dryfoos, 1993, p. 557.)

Although the youth strategies have been running for some years, School Liaison Groups or Joint Assessment Teams have not been formed in all schools. This, however, cannot be solely blamed on head teachers. Social work respondents acknowledged that the success in getting policy agreed had not been matched to the same extent in all local areas and this was attributed to a failure on both sides – social work and education – to give greater priority to working together and to commit resources to joint strategies (Kendrick and Fraser, 1993). McCullough (1991) found that there was wide variation in the way in which school liaison groups operated and while most schools had established a school liaison group, a substantial minority had not established secure and enduring systems for formal liaison between the agencies (McCullough, 1991).

In Tayside Region, the planning process for the Strategy for Young People has taken longer than anticipated. It involved a lot of 'unpacking history', particularly in the relationship between Social Work and Education. The Strategy's development has been punctuated by different perspectives and expectations, so that there has not always been total consensus on the direction it was to take. This process has been particularly evident in the shifting balance between the two main strands of the strategy

– the community development aspect for all young people, and the case decision-making aspect focused on troubled and troublesome young people. The roles of the principal agencies involved in the strategy are different in relation to the two aspects and this has resulted in differing levels of commitment to different aspects of the strategy.

Participants in the local TRYST groups also raised a number of issues. Some respondents considered that the resourcing of the local Strategy groups needed to be given serious consideration, particularly as they developed. The identification of the Strategy with particular secondary schools was also considered to have created certain problems, especially when catchment areas of the schools were wide. In one school pilot area, the strategy was almost totally school-focused since its catchment area was so wide that there was difficulty in creating a community-based focus. In another school, with a wide catchment area, two local sub-groups were set up. However, this meant that there was little activity focused on the school itself. This issue has been addressed in the subsequent development of the strategy.

Supporting families

A good deal of research has shown the effectiveness of parental involvement in schools in improving pupil attainment. In the United States, reviews of empirical studies of academic learning have shown that parents directly or indirectly influence eight chief determinants of cognitive, affective and behavioural learning (Constable and Walberg, 1988, p. 432):

- student ability
- student motivation
- the quality of instruction
- the amount of instruction
- the psychological climate of the class
- academically stimulating home environment
- characteristics of the student's peer groups outside school
- exposure to mass media, in particular, television.

Improving school-home relationships can produce significant effects on learning and school-parent programmes to improve academic conditions in the home have an outstanding record of success in promoting achievement (Topping, 1986; Constable and Walberg, 1988; Marland, 1985; Munn, 1993). In the UK, a number of projects and initiatives have been developed based on the idea of improving partnerships between families and schools (Bastiani, 1988; Bastiani, 1993; Wolfendale, 1989).

In the context of youth strategies, a number of multi-agency initiatives have been developed to support families involving education, social work, police and other agencies. The Castlemilk Education/Social

Work Project in Glasgow aims to prevent pupils from dropping out of school or being excluded. The project is school-based and is multi-disciplinary involving school staff, social workers and an educational psychologist. Focusing on preventive work with first and second year pupils, the project has developed groupwork with pupils on a range of issues. The project has also set up a parents' support group 'to promote positive relationships between parents and school' and its 'main aim is to look at communicating with teenagers'. In order to avoid any stigma, all parents of first year pupils were invited to the group (Webb, 1991).

A recent initiative in supporting families has been developed in one of the local TRYST groups in the Tayside Strategy for Young People. The Kirkton Parents Education and Support Group was developed from a strongly expressed view that parents and voluntary and statutory agencies needed to work together in order to work effectively with young people. The first group began in May 1993 and although only intended to run for twelve weeks it ran for six months. Using a self-help philosophy, the group addressed issues such as parenting skills, drugs, alcohol, crime and sexuality, and dealing with statutory agencies (Tayside Regional Council, 1994).

In Lothian Region, Panmure House provides a joint education and social work provision for young people whose needs are best met within a specialist setting. However, the unit operates on a model which stresses the shared responsibility of educational programmes between Panmure House and the young person's mainstream school. Simpson (1992) reported that:

> ...individual programmes...range from those which allow young people to return to their base school and be presented with Standard grades, to those designed to deal with basic problems in numeracy and literacy. In all cases the co-operation and help we have had from base schools has been of the highest order. (p. 91.)

Young people are encouraged to participate in decision making, both at individual and group levels. Panmure House views work with the families of the young people as an integral part of its service. Through building relationships with families 'it has been possible to challenge the sometimes negative attitudes of the family to formal education' (Simpson, 1991, p. 94).

As the work of Panmure House stressed, an important aspect of supporting families is through their involvement in the process of planning and decision-making. In education, it has been highlighted that pupils with special educational needs and their parents should be fully involved in the planning process (SCCC, 1993). Yet McCullough found that School Liaison Groups rarely involved young people and their parents in decision-making:

> With a few exceptions, children and their families were not invited to attend SLGs, they did not receive information about what had been discussed or

decided by SLGs, and in many cases they were unaware that they and/or their children had been the subject of inter-professional discussion. (McCullough, 1991.)

However, recent research on the Strategy for Young People in Tayside Region, which involved analysis of the minutes of 40 joint education and social work case conferences (distinct from child protection cases conferences) showed a higher level of participation of young people and their parents. Parents attended almost two-thirds of the case conferences and the minutes of another fifth of the meetings indicated that the parents had been invited. Children and young people attended almost half of the case conferences. This proportion increased to almost three-fifths in the case of young people over twelve years of age.

The future of youth strategies

Youth strategies, then, are developing in various ways to support young people and their families. Local authority services in Scotland, however, are in the process of undergoing radical changes. In education, devolved management of schools will involve major changes in the relationship between schools and local authorities (Hartley, 1994). Local government reorganisation in Scotland will result in a larger number of smaller authorities and will have major implications for both social work and education services, particularly in relation to the provision of specialist services (Kendrick, forthcoming).

The Local Government Etc. (Scotland) Bill makes a number of provisions for joint boards, committees and joint contracting arrangements and thus acknowledges the difficulties some of the new authorities will have in providing services on their own. An increase in the number of joint arrangements for the provision of services could lead to a lack of accountability and responsibility and a decrease in public understanding. Kerley and Orr (1993) argue that cross-boundary cooperation between local authorities will be difficult and complex. They also suggest that 'in a 'mixed economy of care' a plethora of providers having to deal with a number of purchasers, or collaborating purchasers with different policy stances, introduces further complexity to already complex areas of policy' (p. 316).

The Local Government Etc. (Scotland) Bill also removes the statutory requirement to have separate Social Work and Education Committees, so some of the new local authorities may decide to establish a single department for both social work and education (Mitchell and Clode, 1993). This almost occurred in one English local authority, where the planned merging of the education and social services departments was only reversed following a change in the political control of the authority (Sone, 1993).

In the context of such change and uncertainty, the positive developments in inter-agency working may be in jeopardy. Elizabeth Maginnis, discussing Lothian Region's Youth Strategy is, however, more optimistic:

> *Taken alongside the increasingly valuable professional relevance of the Strategy, I believe our education system, as a whole, is more predisposed to accept the values and culture implicit in the Youth Strategy which will make its early demise under devolved school management or local government reorganisation easier to predict than to enact.* (Lothian Regional Council, 1994.)

To prevent such an early demise, the agencies involved in supporting families through inter-agency work will need to increase their commitment to joint working. They will all need to accept shared responsibility for the problems of young people and their families and to underpin this responsibility with a joint commitment for resources.

References

Allan, M and Fearon, B. (1989) 'Central Region: A Policy-Led Youth Strategy?' in K. Gill and T. Pickles (eds.) *Active Collaboration: Joint Practice and Youth Strategies.* Glasgow: ITRC.

Audit Commission (1994) *Seen But Not Heard: Co-ordinating Community Child Health and Social Services for Children in Need.* HMSO: London.

Bastiani, J. (ed.) (1988) *From Policy to Practice: Parents and Teachers*, vol 2. Windsor: NFER-Nelson.

Bastiani, J. (1993) 'Parents as Partners: Genuine Progress or Empty Rhetoric?' in P. Munn (ed.) *Parents and Schools: Customers, Managers or Partners.* London: Routledge.

Berridge, D. (1985) *Children's Homes.* Oxford: Basil Blackwell.

Berridge, D. and Cleaver, H. (1987) *Foster Home Breakdown.* Oxford: Basil Blackwell.

Bruce, N. (1983) 'Social Work and Education', in Lishman, J. (ed.) *Collaboration and Conflict: Working with Others*, Research Highlights in Social Work, No. 7. Aberdeen University Press.

Constable, R. and Walberg H. (1988) 'School Social Work: Facilitating Home, School and Community Partnerships', *Urban Education*, Vol 22 No 4, pp. 429 – 443.

Dryfoos, J. (1993) 'Schools as Places for Health, Mental Health, and Social Services', *Teachers College Record*, Vol 94 No 3, pp. 540 – 547.

Gill, K. and Pickles, T. (eds.) (1989) *Active Collaboration: Joint Practice and Youth Strategies.* Glasgow: ITRC.

Hartley, D. (1994) 'Devolved School Management: The 'New Deal' in Scottish Education, *Journal of Education Policy*, Vol 9 No 2, pp. 129 – 140.

HMSO (1966) *Social Work and the Community*, Cmnd 3065. Edinburgh: HMSO.

HMSO (1994) *Children (Scotland) Bill*, London: HMSO.

Jackson, S. (1987) *The Education of Children in Care*, Bristol Papers No. 1, School of Applied Social Studies, University of Bristol.

Jackson, S. (1989) 'Residential Care and Education', *Children & Society*, Vol. 4 No. 2, pp. 335 – 350.

Kearney, B. (1992) *The Report of the Inquiry into Child Care Policies in Fife*. Edinburgh: HMSO.

Kendrick, A. (1986) *Self-Help or Dependency? An Evaluation of Four Projects Working with Local Communities*, Stirling: Aberlour Child Care Trust/Central Regional Council/NCH/Scottish Council for Single Parents.

Kendrick, A. (forthcoming) *Residential Care in the Integration of Child Care Services*, Central Research Unit Papers. The Scottish Office: Edinburgh.

Kendrick, A. and Fraser, S. (1993) *A Study of the Integration of Child Care Services in Scottish Social Work Departments: Report on Stage One*, Report to Social Work Services Group, Scottish Office.

Kerley, R. and Orr, K. (1993) 'Joint Arrangements in Scotland', *Local Government Studies*, Vol 19 No 3, pp. 309 – 318.

Kilbrandon (1964) *The Report of the Committee on Children and Young Persons in Scotland*. Edinburgh: HMSO.

Lockyer, A. (1988) *Study of Children's Hearings' Disposals in Relation to Resources*, Children's Panel Chairmen's Group.

Lothian Regional Council (1994) 'Address by Councillor Elizabeth Maginnis', *Youth Strategy Conference*, Papers and Responses from Contributors to the Youth Strategy Conference held at the Marine Hotel, North Berwick, 11 November 1993. Edinburgh: Lothian Regional Council Department of Education.

Maginnis, E. (1989) 'Lothian Region's Youth Strategy: A Political Perspective', in K. Gill and T. Pickles (eds), *Active Collaboration: Joint Practice and Youth Strategies*. Glasgow: ITRC.

McCullough, D. (1991) *Developing a Strategy: A Study of School Liaison Groups in Central Region*. Glasgow: Jordanhill College.

Mapstone, E. (1983) *Crossing the Boundaries: New Directions in the Mental Health Services for Children and Young People in Scotland*, Report of a Working Group set up by the Mental Disorder Programme Planning Group. Edinburgh: HMSO.

Marland, M. (1985) 'Parents, Schooling, and the Welfare of Pupils', in P. Ribbins (ed.) *Schooling and Welfare*. Lewes: The Falmer Press.

Mitchell, D. and Clode, D. (1993) Uncertain Footing, *Community Care*, 21 October 1993.

Munn, P. (1993) 'Introduction' in P. Munn (ed.) *Parents and Schools: Customers, Managers or Partners*. London: Routledge.

Pickles, T. (1992) 'Youth Strategies in Scotland' in G. Lloyd (ed.) *Chosen with Care? Responses to Disturbing and Disruptive Behaviour*. Edinburgh: Moray House Publications

Russell, L. (1989) 'Strathclyde Region: The Development of Policies for Working with Young People at Risk', in K. Gill and T. Pickles (eds.) *Active Collaboration: Joint Practice and Youth Strategies*. Glasgow: ITRC.

SCCC (1993) *Special Educational Needs within the 5–14 Curriculum: Support for Learning*. Dundee: Scottish Consultative Council on the Curriculum.

Schaffer, M. (1992) 'Children's Hearings' in G. Lloyd (ed.) *Chosen with Care? Responses to Disturbing and Disruptive Behaviour*. Edinburgh: Moray House Publications

Scottish Office (1990) *Review of Child Care Law in Scotland*, Report of a Review Group Appointed by the Secretary of State. Edinburgh: HMSO.

Scottish Office (1993) *Scotland's Children: Proposals for Child Care Policy and Law.* Edinburgh: HMSO.

Simpson, D. (1991) 'Panmure House School Groups: One Approach to Dealing with Young People's Schooling Difficulties', in G. Lloyd (ed.) *Chosen with Care? Responses to Disturbing and Disruptive Behaviour.* Edinburgh: Moray House Publications.

Smrekar, C. (1993) 'Rethinking Family-School Interactions: A Prologue to Linking Schools and Social Services', *Education and Urban Society*, Vol 25 No 2, pp. 175 – 186.

Sone, K. (1993) 'Split Decision', *Community Care*, 21 October 1993.

Tayside Regional Council (1994) *Tayside Strategy for Young People Update.* Dundee: Tayside Regional Council.

Topping, K. (1986) *Parents as Educators: Training Parents to Teach their Children.* London: Croom Helm.

Webb, S. (1991) 'School's In', *Social Work Today,* 24 January 1991, pp. 13 – 15.

Welton, J. (1985) 'Schools and a Multi-Professional Approach to Welfare' in P. Ribbins (ed.) *Schooling and Welfare.* Lewes: The Falmer Press.

Wolfendale, S. (ed.) (1989) *Parental Involvement: Developing Networks Between School, Home and Community.* London: Cassell Educational Limited.

10

SUPPORT TO FAMILIES: DILEMMAS, CHANGES AND CHALLENGES

Malcolm Hill, Rosalind Hawthorne Kirk and Diana Part

THIS final section does not attempt to summarise the preceding chapters – readers are referred to the Preface for that purpose. Instead we draw together some of the themes from the different contributions as we review the current role of the state in relation to families.

Social support – social control

The book has attempted to review current policies at central and local levels which affect families with dependent children. It has ranged widely across varied types of family, forms of service and professional perspectives, but each chapter has given attention to families' needs and actual or potential responses to those needs. Particular emphasis has been given to the systematic evidence available from research and from the critical analysis of official information. The issues considered have been applicable across the UK, but we have included several chapters which focus on the situation in Scotland and also comparative material about the rest of Western Europe.

The common thread has been the notion that the rearing of children is a vital enterprise which is shared between families and the wider community. Parents and children themselves normally take on the major part of that responsibility and they are entitled to considerable autonomy in doing so. In addition assistance needs to be available from outside services and professionals, sometimes on a universal basis recognising common needs and interests (as with schools), sometimes of a more specialised kind to meet particular circumstances.

The importance of central and local government services in supporting families has been a central rationale for the book, but this is neither uncontested nor straightforward. It is worth mentioning at the outset that words themselves can evoke feelings for and against. The 'state' or 'government' can be portrayed as inhuman, insensitive, or simply incompetent. It is not necessary to look to such extremes as Nazi Germany or the Stalinist Soviet Union to realise that governments can be experienced as oppressive by all, many or some citizens. Yet no modern society operates without a government and, at their best, state institutions represent the aspirations of social groupings of more positive connotation – the people, society or – perhaps most hallowed terms of all – the community or nation.

The idea of a widely available range of services provided by 'the state' (i.e. society or community) is at odds with *laissez-faire* approaches to family policy and child care policy, themselves rooted in wider attitudes about the economy and society (Harding, 1991). Those who argue for a residual role for the state concentrated only on a minority suggest that comprehensive services are costly (which they are), but also unnecessary or undermining of individual and parental responsibility (which is more contentious). Halsey (1993) observed that policies needed to adapt to new circumstances (including greater equality and choice for women, demographic changes) but have done so in a manner which exacerbates rather than ameliorates family difficulties:

> *The much needed reform of the system required comprehensive strengthening of supporting health, education and security services if quality children were to be produced, women to have freedom to combine motherhood with career, and men were to be encouraged to take fuller part in their domestic rearing of offspring. Instead the evidence of more recent changes is that supporting services have deteriorated, the increment of economic growth has been transferred disproportionately to the individual pocket horizontally and to the rich vertically by the running down of family allowances, the raising of national insurance contributions, the abandoning of joint taxation for spouses, the failure to fund adequate community care and so on.* (p. 68.)

An alternative response is that an array of financial and practical services are necessary to compensate for the risks of a complex urbanised society in which for growing numbers of citizens there is increasing uncertainty about the long-term prospects for stable well-paid employment and hence self-reliance. Services such as early years provision can represent an investment with eventual financial pay-offs, whether in terms of individuals' greater skills and earning power or reduced costs to the community related to truancy and crime (Hawthorne Kirk, Chapter 7). That has been one of the reasons why other countries in Western Europe have more generous universal payments for children and more extensive day care services than in the UK (Hill, Chapter 2). Other factors have included commitment to choice, gender equality and social solidarity.

Even so the role of the state in relation to families is not confined to positive assistance. Marshall (Chapter 5) refers to the 'social policing role' of social workers, teachers, health visitors and others. Perhaps three aspects of this can be separated.

(i) *'Protective' surveillance* The first aspect concerns the role of society regarding the welfare of all its children. There is common acceptance that the state does have a duty to intervene in family life in order to protect children from dangers and hazards, either when their own parents are unable to do so or when the parents themselves are the source of risk through neglect or active abuse (Archard, 1993). In order to do this, there have to be systems for monitoring children by professionals (e.g. medical checks) and for responding to concerns by members of the public about children's welfare. State actions in this capacity may well be supportive to children, but are experienced as surveillance or coercion by parents. This highlights the view that families should not be treated as unitary entities. The interest of a child may differ from and conflict with the intentions or actions of the child's parent. The interest and wishes of two parents in the same family can also diverge.

(ii) *'Protective' intervention* When representatives of the state are concerned about a child, the manner of intervention can be supportive or coercive, or indeed a combination of both. In the UK (and in North America) legalistic responses have become predominant over the last twenty years (Parton, 1991), with an emphasis on investigation with a view to proving cases and obtaining orders in court (or at a children's hearing in Scotland). Moreover access to services has often come to be contingent on assessment of risk and often accompanied by legal sanctions (Gibbons, chapter 6). Sadly, in such a complex field it is difficult to identify risk situations without frequent errors (Dingwall, 1989). As a result many needy families face the indignity of investigation yet receive no positive support afterwards because they become 'low priority cases' when ill-treatment is not confirmed. This contrasts with the stances in France and the Netherlands which are based much more on voluntary cooperation with parents (Chapter 2). The latter approach lessens many of the antagonisms and suspicions of families towards the authorities, although a disadvantage could be that more children in those systems are not adequately sheltered from ill-treatment.

A further problem is to determine what are the circumstances in which such intervention is justified and how broad or narrow they should be. Judgements about this have varied greatly in time and place, as illustrated by attitudes to infanticide and corporal punishment. Revelations about child sexual abuse in the last ten years have dramatically altered perceptions of the extent of ill-treatment within families, even if there remains uncertainty and disagreement about the precise incidence (Gillham, 1991).

(iii) *Pervasive influence* Post-modernist commentators have suggested that the global enterprise of present-day professionals is tainted, not only when they are conscious of the social control role as in child protection but also when they see themselves as acting benignly (Donzelot, 1980; Howe, 1994). The argument is that medical, educational and other professionals exercise informal power over families on behalf of the state. Even health visitors who are often well regarded by parents as helpful advisers can also be seen as 'indoctrinating' them with prevailing and changeable views about proper upbringing. All professionals in contact with families influence individuals and families. From this perspective, they are regarded as determining or 'scripting' how they think about issues of parenting, childhood and abuse. They also act as moral arbiters in deciding when particular ways of life and upbringing are acceptable or not. Their power derives from their presumed expertise, in the eyes of lay people and in legal settings. Thus, radiologists and paediatricians played a significant part in the social construction of physical abuse of children as a social problem and (feminist) social workers in the creation of sexual abuse as a public issue (Parton, 1985; Evans, 1994). Whilst it is helpful to be aware of the ability of professional groups to impose their definitions and explanations of phenomena, especially on less articulate and confident people, it is also the case that politicians, the media and other interest groups all play active parts. Members of the public are not all passive and can contribute individually and collectively, too.

Welfare pluralism

The state has never had a monopoly in assisting or controlling families. Besides the important role of informal social networks (Kirk, Chapter 7), voluntary organisations have always been important, including the NSPCC and RSSPCC whose former uniforms were more akin to those of the police than any public employee's apparel. Indeed voluntary agencies were at the heart of responses to poverty, crime and family disruption in the 19th Century. Since the establishment of the Welfare state they have continued to provide substantial services, often of a more innovatory and specialist nature (Heywood, 1978; Hendrick, 1992). Several of these agencies were at the forefront of the development of multi-purpose family centres, for example (Holman, 1988; Stones, 1993).

The 1980s witnessed a decided shift in policy and practice in favour of what came to be termed welfare pluralism (Johnson, 1990). There has been a political attack on public provision from governments advocating individualism, family responsibility and choice – values which are held by many parents themselves (Jordan, Redley and James, 1994). The scope of services provided by non-profit voluntary bodies and increasingly private, profit-making agencies has been enhanced by such measures as the Under-fives Initiative of the mid-1980s and competitive tendering. The role of local authorities has shifted in many respects from that of direct provision to enabling and supporting voluntary bodies and increasingly also the independent (profit-making) sector. This trend has been most apparent in adult services, but has been evident in pre-school provision for some time too (Pugh, 1988). A number of authorities have reorganised their children and family services along a purchaser-provider split or case management-service divide in imitation of community care arrangements.

There have also been twin intellectual attacks on the welfare state. The New Right perceives public spending as a restraint on the market's ability to raise living standards and public services as limiting choice (Anderson, 1986). From a different viewpoint, postmodernists question the success of the rational approach to social problems embodied in the liberal welfare state and argue that the main beneficiaries have been the professionals and bureaucrats it employs rather than service users (Hewitt, 1994).

There are certainly benefits in having a range of services and choice. Gibbons (Chapter 6) describes the positive effects of agencies like Homestart and Newpin, some of which developed from self-help initiatives with the advantage of high user involvement and control. However there are also dangers of segregation and exclusion, especially when access to core services becomes severely rationed (Kirk and Part, Chapter 1).

Government policies of community care have also been predicated on the assumption that there is a large untapped reserve of informal support. In practice this has typically meant support by women, although this is less true for care by spouses in old age (Finch and Groves, 1983; Finch and Mason, 1993; Fisher, 1994). Much more than men, women are still expected to feel greater responsibility for any dependent family member at the expense of their careers and other personal interests. Ironically, this idea relies on the notion of social obligation which is at odds with the individualism central to other policy areas. Community care has mostly been discussed in relation to elderly people and adults with disabilities or mental health problems, though it is relevant to children who are disabled or have chronic health conditions. Also we need to be aware that when talking about the capacity of the 'community' to care, not only do many adult carers need support and sometimes relief, but some carers are children themselves. They often cope in silence at considerable cost to their education and social lives (Aldridge and Becker, 1994). Another group of children with major needs are those whose childhoods are blighted by their parents' addiction to alcohol or drugs. Some of these children are very resilient and capable, whilst many do gain significant help from their extended families and friends. Nonetheless, external assistance is also often required, for example through practical help with domestic tasks, counselling or additional schooling,

The proliferation of agencies can also make the perennial problem of collaboration and coordination more difficult, especially when combined with the effects of opting out (schools and health services) and re-organisation of local government (Kirk and Part, Chapter 1; Kendrick, Chapter 9). Co-ordinating bodies then grapple with the difficulties of understanding and reconciling varied structures, roles, remits, attitudes and statuses (Hallett and Birchall, 1992). Users may be deterred by the increased complexity of gaining access to appropriate services.

Partnership and participation

It is not just the nature and availability of services for families which matter. How they are experienced and shaped by users is also of great concern. Traditionally most services have been 'top-down' – planned, managed and run by the service-providers according to their ideas about needs and appropriate responses. Patients have had little or no say in deciding the purpose and nature of hospitals or clinics, pupils or parents in the running of schools, perhaps least of all claimants in the delivery of social security. This is changing, even if more at the level of rhetoric and less in practical terms. From different parts of the political spectrum, the rights of people as consumers or as citizens have been championed.

This can be complicated when families are considered. As the issues like domestic violence and post-divorce child support have illustrated, the interests of mothers and fathers can diverge. Similarly, parents and children do not always see eye to eye and then how are parents' and children's rights to be balanced? Parents and their children can have different expectations, wishes and criteria for judging a service (Hill, Triseliotis and Borland, Chapter 8). In education, several measures have been introduced at national level to increase the influence of parents, but virtually none to enhance pupil involvement.

In England and Wales the Children Act of 1989 (implemented in 1991) was heralded as a major step forward as regards both partnership with parents and participation by children. Although it was broader in scope than previous Children Acts, this legislation was still not truly for all children, as it concentrates mainly on children in difficulties or with special needs. Thus it largely affects the work of social services and not of other key agencies concerned with children such as education. It broke new ground in integrating private law (to do with divorce and separation) and public law (relating to local authority supervision and care). In many respects it was a masterly act of compromise and acquired all party support. The protective powers of local authorities were enhanced in some respects (albeit with greater court controls), whilst deference was made to the position of both parents and children. The concept of parental rights was largely substituted by that of parental responsibility, whilst the need to ascertain and take account of children's wishes was strengthened. The ambiguity has meant that in some circumstances the Act has been used to resist a child's wish to leave home (because the parents should be responsible), whilst in others it has been interpreted that children's requests to be accommodated by a local authority must be acceded to, even if the child's parents oppose.

At the time of writing (February 1995), Scotland has not experienced equivalent changes in child and family law, although it is expected that the Children (Scotland) Bill will be enacted in the next year. In spite of the very different Scottish tradition in this field (Marshall, Chapter 5) it appears that the new Act will be much affected by the English experience. Whereas the preceding White Paper stressed the significance of children's rights and referred favourably to the UN Convention on children's rights, there is no explicit mention of these in the Bill. However, it does stipulate that children should be consulted about any major decision (according to their age and understanding) and parents should also be involved too (Kendrick, Chapter 9). This is potentially a major step forward for children's participation in a wide range of settings, including home and school. With the growth of children's rights officers, children's charters and shared agreements and reviews, the issue now is not so much whether children are consulted, but the more subtle one of enabling them to express their views fully and participate effectively to ensure that their involvement is not tokenistic (Triseliotis et al., 1995).

Continuity and change in families

Policies and services must adapt to changing circumstances. We have much more information than ever before about families, but interpreting the meaning and implications remains a difficult and subjective process. Recent views have tended to polarise between those who bemoan the perceived decline of 'the family' or of parental responsibility and those who champion more freedom and diversity (Dennis and Erdos, 1992; Dallos and Sapsford, 1995). As Richards carefully showed in Chapter 3, it is important to acknowledge but not exaggerate changes and to recognise that these can bring both gains and problems. The majority of people do still marry and the majority of marriages do persist, but it is also true that compared with the 1940s though not necessarily earlier eras there are fewer people living together 'in wedlock' and significantly greater tendency for individuals to progress to second or third marriages.

We are still struggling with the legal, social and financial consequences of this. That has been most evident in relation to the Child Support Agency. There is widespread acceptance of the principle that parents separated from their children (most often fathers) should continue to provide financial support and to remain involved in other ways. This is not always easy to reconcile with the needs of children in a second family (Gibson, 1994). So far the UK does not seem to have found as good way of doing this as some countries in Scandinavia and elsewhere (Hill, Chapter 2). There is also a continuing debate in agencies concerned with family separation (such as mediation services) about how far involvement in decisions about their care and access is a child's right or a burden which should be assumed by the adults (Marshall, Chapter 5).

Recent studies all indicate that many families have higher standards of living than heretofore, but increasing proportions are being left behind (Long, Chapter 4; Kumar, 1993; Alcock, 1994). Increased unemployment and restrictions on benefits are largely responsible for this. Only national and indeed international policies can redress that situation, but as both Chapters 4 and 7 showed local projects can enable some families to overcome poverty through providing child care, training and employment opportunities. Increasingly and like other family policy matters, this has become an issue with international as well as national dimensions and influences. The Commission monitoring the implementation of the UN Convention on the Rights of the Child has berated the UK for the substantial increases in child poverty and begging. The European Union has also committed itself to the alleviation of poverty and sponsored a small number of employment training and day-care schemes in its Poverty-3 programme. It is mostly when poverty and family instability are combined that risks of children being placed in public care are greatly increased (Bebbington and Miles, 1989). This indicates the need for extra help to be available alongside more general services, a blending of community and client-based approaches as depicted in relation to young children and adolescents in Chapters 7 and 9 respectively.

In the approach to the twenty-first century we are beholden to consider carefully the implications of technological developments just as much as demographic changes. Inevitably families will be at the heart of these transformations which are opening up the home to external communication of many kinds and which can radically alter the way people shop, work, play, learn and maintain personal relationships. The increasing access to computer games, videos, mobile phones, fax machines etc. has already greatly affected the nature of leisure and work, at least for those families privileged to include someone in paid employment. As with most innovations, there are opportunities for greater freedom and personal fulfilment, but also potential for individuals and perhaps especially children to be exploited, neglected or harmed. Working parents can spend more time at home and, in theory, be more available to their children. The participative rights of children may be extended by their increased access to and control over learning and communication materials, though some adults fear children's protective rights may be reduced by their early exposure to frightening or exploitative videos.

It is important that we do not let statistics related to family and household composition or material circumstances dominate our view of family life. We need also to understand the processes involved. Cohabitation of parents may be experienced by a child to be as stable and loving as marriage. Children can be as deeply distressed by conflict between parents living together as by the consequences of separation. They are not simply passive recipients of negative influences from the TV, video and computer. An implicit theme of this volume has been that policy should be grounded in detailed research. Each chapter has either reviewed a range of relevant studies or reported in detail on one particular investigation. Policy proposals, policy-making and commentaries thereon involve value choices and dilemmas which research cannot resolve, but it can help ensure that the beliefs and assumptions are based on accurate and precise understanding. There is a need for more systematic knowledge about the everyday lives and experiences of families to complement the wealth of abstract figures and considerable evidence about 'problematic' families. It is also vital that these represent the perspectives not only of adults, but of children and young people too (Mayall, 1994). Likewise, it is important to understand the nature of family relationships in the context of their social networks and the localities where they live. Community life has not died in the face of technological and social changes at work and at home – it has simply evolved and diversified (Crow and Allan, 1994).

Meeting the challenges

In recent years, services and policies which support families have been subject to the same re-examination and reconstitution as other parts of the welfare state. The demographic, material, employment and technological contexts have changed and it is not possible nor desirable to return to the previous status quo. The manner in which families and other social agents share the task of upbringing is changing and must continue to adapt. It remains true however that the wider society has an interest and obligation to promote the life chances of children through supporting parents and parental figures. By investing in families, society invests in its own future.

Structures and processes of supports should be based on careful assessment and review of circumstances and needs, as well as systematic evaluation of what works well and what works less well. One of the major gains of recent years has been the emphasis on user participation, particularly in relation to adults but gradually as regards children too. Services need to be designed and run with substantial involvement of users and other stakeholders. Only in this way can they be truly responsive to families' needs and wishes.

References

Alcock, P. (1994) *Understanding Poverty.* London: Macmillan.
Aldridge, J. and Becker, S. (1994) *Children Who Care.* Loughborough, University of Loughborough.
Anderson, D. (1986) *Family Portraits,* Social Affairs Unit, London.

Archard, D. (1993) *Children: Rights and Childhood.* London, Routledge.
Bebbington, A. and Miles, J. (1989) 'The background of children who enter Local Authority Care', *British Journal of Social Work,* 19, 5, 349–358.
Crow, G. and Allan, G. (1994) *Community Life.* London: Harvester Wheatsheaf.
Dallos, R. and Sapsford, R. (1995) 'Patterns of diversity and lived realities', in J. Muncie, M. Wetherell, R. Dallos ad A. Cochrane, *Understanding the Family.* London: Sage.
Dennis, N. and Erdos, G. (1992) *Families without Fatherhood.* London: IEA Health and Welfare Unit.
Dingwall, R. (1989) 'Some problems about predicting child abuse and neglect' in O. Stevenson (ed.) *Child Abuse,* Hemel Hempstead, Harvester Wheatsheaf.
Donzelot, J. (1980) *Policing the Family.* London: Hutchinson.
Evans, D. (1994) "Falling angels? The material construction of children as sexual citizens', *International Journal of Children's Rights,* 2, 1–33.
Finch, J. and Groves, D. (1983) *A Labour of Love.* London: RKP.
Finch, J, and Mason, J. (1993) *Negotiating Family Responsibilities.* London: Tavistock/Routledge.
Fisher, M. (1994) 'Man-made care: Community care and older male carers', *British Journal of Social Work,* 24, 659–680.
Gibson, C, S. (1994) *Dissolving Wedlock.* London: Routledge.
Gillham, B. (1991) *The Facts about Child Sexual Abuse.* London: Cassell.
Hallett, C. and Birchall, J. (1992) *Coordination and Child Protection: A Review of the Literature.* Edinburgh: H.M.S.O.
Halsey, A. H. (1993) 'Changes in the family', in G. Pugh (ed.) *30 Years of Change for Children.* London: National Children's Bureau.
Harding, L. F. (1991) *Perspectives in Child Care Policy.* London: Longman.
Hendrick, H. (1992) *Child Welfare: England 1872–1989.* London: Routledge.
Hewitt, M. (1994) 'Social policy and the question of postmodernism', in R. Page and J. Baldock (eds.) *Social Policy Review 6.* Canterbury: Social Policy Association.
Heywood, J. (1978) *Children in Care.* London: Routledge & Kegan Paul.
Holman, R. (1988) *Putting Families First.* London: Macmillan.
Howe, D. (1994) 'Modernity, postmodernity and social work', *British Journal of Social Work,* 24, 513–532.
Johnson, N, (1990) *Reconstructing the Welfare State.* Hemel Hempstead, Harvester Wheatsheaf.
Jordan, B., Redley, M. and James, S. (1994) *Putting the Family First.* London, UCL Press.
Kumar, V. (1993) *Poverty and Inequality in the UK: The Effects on Children.* London: National Children's Bureau.
Mayall, B. (ed.) (1994) *Children's Childhoods Observed and Experienced.* London: Falmer Press.
Parton, N. (1985) *The Politics of Child Abuse.* London: Macmillan.
Parton, N. (1991) *Governing the Family.* London: Macmillan.
Pugh, G. (1988) *Services for Under Fives.* London, National Children's Bureau.
Stones, C. (1994) *Family Centres in Action.* London: Macmillan.
Triseliotis, J., Borland, M. , Hill, M. and Lambert, L. (1995) *Teenagers and Social Work Services.* London: H.M.S.O.

INDEX

Abortion 22
Accommodated children see children in care
Access (between parents and children) 73, 129, 155-6
Access to services (by families) xv, 3, 4, 7, 11, 28, 30, 64, 68, 100, 114, 150, 153
Adolescence 12, 41, 119
Adult education 10, 64, 92-3
Afro-Caribbean families 41
Advanced maintenance 27-8
Advocacy 76, 82, 84
Alcohol abuse 90, 153
Amtmand 28
Ante-natal services 9, 20
Anti-poverty strategies 65-6
Area Child Protection Committees 88
Assessing outcomes see Outcomes
Association of Directors of Social Work 83
Audit Commission 8, 89
Australia 27, 51
Austria 17, 19, 23

Bangladeshi families 41
Brazil 66
Befriending 94, 122, 123, 132
Belgium 20, 24, 25, 26, 27, 29, 30
Benefit changes 59, 66
Benefits trap 67
Birth order 25, 26
Birth rates 18, 40, 47
Black families see Ethnic minority families
Bullying 129

Car travel 6, 7, 109
Care in the community, care by the community 8, 12, 153
Case conferences 89, 91, 140, 144
Castlemilk 143
Census 1991 65, 104, 107

Central Government (see also Government intervention) 4, 12, 13, 24, 33, 64
 - role in early years provision 11, 18, 20, 21, 23, 24, 115
Central Region 139
Centralisation 4, 11, 13
Child abuse see Child protection
Child advocates 75, 76
Child bearing 7, 27, 40, 41, 45, 46, 47
Child benefit (see also Family Allowances) 13, 59, 150
Child Care Act 1980 87
Child care (child welfare) 11, 119-30
Child care (day care) facilities 11, 18, 20, 21, 23, 24, 28, 29, 33, 43, 47, 48, 61, 65, 66, 67, 88, 92-3, 95, 99-117, 152
Child care law 3, 11, 12, 72-4, 79, 80-93, 87, 88, 89, 90, 96, 101, 135-7, 154, 155
Child development 20, 29, 66, 82-3, 90, 102, 109, 112, 119
Childminders 29, 90, 100
Child Parent Enrichment Project 95
Child poverty see Poverty,
Child protection xv, 3, 12, 21, 22, 27, 30, 71, 74-5, 79, 81, 83, 84, 87-96, 102, 105, 121, 151, 154
Child Protection Registers 89-91
Child rearing 43, 48
Child sexual abuse 79, 90, 151
Child support 23, 37
Child Support Agency 5, 27, 28, 34, 47, 155
Child tax allowances 18, 26
Childline 22
Children
  Children at risk 3, 12, 20, 30, 87-96, 103, 114, 151
  Children in care 30, 120, 122, 124, 129-31, 137-8

159

Children, *continued*
  Children in need 29, 64, 87-90, 101
  Children looked after see Children in care
  Children's behaviour 11, 119, 121, 126, 132
  Children's health 8, 20, 27, 61-2, 89, 121
  Children's hearings system 11, 12, 71-5, 79, 81, 83, 136, 151
  Children's interests 73, 75, 81, 83, 87, 90, 96, 151
  Children's needs 2, 87, 90
  Children's panels see Children's hearings system
  Children's rights xiv, 2, 10, 21, 31, 66, 73, 81, 82, 83, 135-6, 155, 156
  Children's views 71, 73, 75-6, 80-1, 83, 119-22, 126-31
  Children's welfare 72, 73, 82, 87, 90, 96, 151
  Children with special needs 10, 29, 93-4
  Costs of rearing children 5, 19, 43, 48, 54, 59
Children Act, 1989 xv, 3, 11, 87, 88, 89, 90, 96, 101, 154
Children (Scotland) Bill 3, 12, 135, 155
Church organisations 139
Church, role in family policy 21, 22, 24
Client-focused centres 105, 106, 113-5
Clyde Report 12, 78, 79, 80, 83
Cohabitation 40-7, 156
Collaboration between agencies 10, 11, 78, 88, 101, 124, 132, 135-6, 153
Community care 7, 8, 12, 153
Community development 64, 67, 139, 140, 146
Community development centres 105, 106
Community education 140
Community initiatives 64-8, 69-70, 91
Companionate marriage 44
Compensatory services 90, 91, 95
Compulsory measures 72, 75, 76, 77, 78, 81, 84, 126
Confederation of Family Organisations in the European Community 33
Confidential Doctors 30
Consumerism 9, 64, 156-7
Contraception 31, 41, 46

Coordination (See also Collaboration; Inter-agency work) 88, 105, 135, 136, 141, 153
Coopersmith scale 121, 125, 130
Costs (of rearing children) 5, 19, 43, 48, 54, 59
Council housing 6, 41, 59
Counselling 82, 91, 124
Courts 12, 74, 79, 80, 82
Crime 11, 12, 30, 90, 121, 127, 128, 132
Curator ad litem 73
Custody (of children) 73

Day care see Child care (day care) facilities
Day nurseries 91, 93, 100
Debt 61, 64
Decentralisation of services 30
Decision-making (by social workers) 89, 135, 155
Delinquency see Juvenile crime
Demographic features (of UK population) 40-5, 50-1, 156
Demographic changes 40-1, 47, 150, 155
Denmark 20, 26, 27, 28, 29, 31
'Dependency culture' 60
Department of Health 87, 89, 119, 120
Developmental delay 110, 113
Diet 43, 61, 63
Disability 3, 29, 60, 87, 88, 109
Disadvantage, disadvantaged families 3, 5, 7, 8, 9, 10, 41, 60, 61, 63, 90, 92-93, 107-8, 121-2
Discretionary payments 56, 59
Diversion 30, 75, 76, 120, 124, 133, 139
Divorce 22, 27, 28, 39, 44-5, 46, 48, 73, 82, 154
Doctors 91, 140, 151, 152
Domestic roles 2, 7, 45, 65, 67
Domestic violence 6, 154
Drug abuse 91, 128, 153

Early learning 20, 28, 66
Early years provision xv, 11, 28-9, 93, 99-117, 150, 152
  Hours of opening 106
  Range of early years provision 66, 100, 105, 113, 152
  Review of early years provision 100, 115
  Social support 102, 112

Economic policies 2, 5, 32, 42, 48, 49, 56
Edinburgh 61
Education (see also Schools: Special education) 9-10, 28, 62-3, 143
    Educational attainments (children's) 10, 62, 66, 120, 121
    Educational problems (children's) 10, 137, 138
    Education: parental involvement 9, 154
    Education and poverty 62-3
    Education policy 9, 10, 28, 62
    Education: pupil involvement 154
    Education services, departments 10, 124, 144, 154
    Education and social services 12, 30, 79, 124, 132, 135-47
Educational disadvantage 9, 10, 62, 138
Educational psychologists 139, 140, 143
Emergency protection 79-81
Employment (See also Gender equality; Women's paid employment) 31, 32, 33, 42, 43, 56-8, 61, 65, 66, 156
Empowerment 3, 9, 65-6
England & Wales 3, 10, 11, 12, 51, 61, 77, 87-8, 101, 119
Equal opportunities see Gender equality
Equalisation of burdens 19
Ethnic minorities 3, 40, 45, 60
    - and access to services 3, 29, 107
    - and poverty 60
    - and unemployment 43
    - demographic features 41
European Community 1, 17-34, 41, 47, 156
European Commission 31-3, 51
European Court 32
European Parliament 32, 33
European Poverty Programme 32, 156
European Social Fund 32, 67
European Union 1, 17-34, 41, 156
Examination results 9, 10
Exclusion from schools 10
Explicit family policies 17, 24
Extra-marital births 40-1, 46

Families 1, 3, 39, 56, 65, 92-3, 107-8, 113-4, 121-2
Family allowances 13, 19, 20, 21, 24, 25, 26, 32, 59, 150
Family budgets 20, 24, 63-4, 66

Family centres 23, 32, 64, 88, 91, 93, 95, 99-117, 152
Family change 39-49, 155
Family conflict 3, 27, 75-6, 81, 82, 121, 154, 156
Family Credit 19, 41, 55, 57, 65
Family debts see Debts
Family Impact Statements 23
Family incomes 19, 23, 108
Family law 5, 7, 8, 9, 11, 12, 32, 71-84, 87-90, 135
Family life 18, 22, 39-40, 42, 48, 49, 63, 82, 156
Family planning 31, 41, 46
Family policy xiii, xiv, 17-30, 64
    Family policy aims 4, 18-22, 23
    Family policy mechanisms 17, 18
    Family policy models 22-5, 150, 156
Family poverty see Poverty
Family privacy 3, 22, 40, 42, 48, 71, 82, 100, 101
Family size 25, 26
Family support xiii, 1, 17, 87-90, 112-4
    Meaning of family support 72, 81, 82, 87-8
Family support services 18, 64, 82-3, 87-90, 92-6, 104, 112-4
Family values 3, 22, 39, 40, 45, 71, 155-6
Fathers 5, 106, 112, 155
Feminism 33, 152
Fertility 41, 46, 47
Fife Inquiry see Kearney Report
Financial payments for families 5, 6, 18-9, 25, 61, 65, 92
Finland 17, 21
Fiscal policy (see also Taxation, tax relief) 20, 26, 59
Financial support to families 5, 6, 18-9, 25, 61, 65, 92
Food see Nutrition
Foster care, foster families 31, 74, 120, 122, 123, 130-2
France 18, 19, 20, 21, 22, 24, 25, 26, 27, 28, 29, 30, 151

Gatekeeping 89, 120
Gender differences 45, 57
Gender equality 2, 3, 18, 20, 21, 22, 23, 26, 27, 28, 32, 45, 65, 66, 150
General Health Questionnaire (GHQ) 109
General Household Survey 43

Germany 17, 19, 22, 26, 29
Glasgow 61, 62, 63, 65
Greece 17, 19, 22, 26, 29, 41
Group work 122, 123, 132
Government intervention - ideas about 4, 33, 151-2
Government role (see also Central Government; State-family relationships) 4, 12, 13, 17-34, 100, 151-2

Hardship payments 56
Health (of children) 23, 61-2, 66, 104, 125
Health (in families) 64, 109-111
Health policy 8
Health promotion 9, 10, 68, 109
Health services 7, 8, 61, 89, 153
Health trusts 8
Health visitors 8, 91, 94, 110, 150, 152
Helplines 22
'High risk' families 94
Holland see Netherlands
Home-Start 93-4, 153
Homelessness 5, 6, 122
Households below average income 53-4
Household incomes 5, 18, 19, 41, 57, 108-9
Housing 6, 41, 59
Housing allowances, benefit 19
Housing costs 23, 55
Housing policy 6

Illness see Sick children; Health
Implicit family policies 17, 24
Income maintenance 5, 19, 24, 25, 43
Income support 18, 55-6, 59, 61, 65
  Exclusion of 16-17 year olds 5, 56
Indian families 41
Individualism 3, 4, 5, 71, 152
Inequalities 3, 5, 6, 8, 9, 10, 18, 32, 59, 62
Informal helping, support 101-4,124,153
Inter-agency work xv, 10, 11, 30, 88, 89, 124, 135-48
Internal markets 4, 7
International Year of the Child 71
International Year of the Family xiii, 34, 51, 71
Internationalisation of family support 31-3
Investigation (in child protection) 78, 80, 89-90

Ireland 17, 21, 22, 241 29, 31
Italy 22, 23, 26, 29, 30, 41

Juge des Enfants 22, 30
Juvenile crime (see also Crime; Welfare approaches) 11, 12, 30, 74, 76, 121, 127, 128, 132

Kearney Report 75, 120, 138
Kilbrandon Report 74, 136
Kin(ship) 39, 44, 45, 100, 102, 103, 111
Kirkton 143

Labour market 2, 5, 18, 21, 56-7, 60
Law and the family see Family law
Lawyers 79
Leaving care 122, 123, 128, 133
Legal representation 76, 81, 82
Legislation (and family policy) 5, 7, 8, 9, 11, 12, 17, 32, 144, 154
Literacy 62, 93
Living standards 59, 156
Local authority housing 6, 41, 59
Local authority services 4, 6, 7, 8, 9, 10, 11, 12, 30, 87, 88, 89, 100, 104, 115, 119-20, 132, 138, 152-3
Local government reorganisation 144, 153
Lone parents 20, 22, 24, 25, 26, 27, 29, 32, 42, 104, 107, 109, 113
  - and poverty 20, 24, 43, 49, 60, 65
Lothian Region 139, 143, 145
Low pay 56-7, 60, 66
Luxembourg 17, 20, 22, 23, 24, 25, 28, 29

Maltreatment of children (see also Child protection) 90-2
Market approaches in the public sector 4, 6-8, 9, 10, 11, 12
Marital separation 41, 42, 73, 155
Marriage(s) 40-2, 44, 45, 155
Maternity leave 21, 27
Matrimonial Proceedings (Scotland) Act 1958 73
Maturity (of a child) 82-3
Means testing 26, 106
Mediation 73, 82, 125, 155
Mediterranean countries 24, 31, 41
Migration 32-3
Ministries for families 23, 33
Mixed economy of welfare 4, 6, 7, 8, 11, 30, 114, 115, 152-4

162

INDEX

Models of family policy 22-5
Monitoring (of children, of families) 12, 21, 77-8, 91, 96
Monogamy 44, 47, 48
Mothers 6, 19, 45, 46, 65-7, 106, 107
Mount Hope Family Centre 95
Multi-disciplinary collaboration 29-30, 88, 141

Natalism 18, 21, 26
National Child Development Study 62
National Curriculum 10
National Health Service 7-9
NHS and Community Care Act, 1990 7, 8, 12
National Insurance 2, 29, 59
Neglect (of children) 71, 90, 95-6
Neighbourhood centres 102, 105, 106, 113, 114
Neighbourhood Watch 11
Netherlands 18, 20, 23, 25, 26, 27, 28, 29, 30, 31, 151
Network on Child Care 33
Networking 31, 32, 33, 102
Newpin 94, 95, 153
Northern Ireland 2 9, 39, 51
Norway 17, 20, 23, 24, 25, 27
Nuclear families 2, 44, 45, 47
Nurseries see Day nurseries; Nursery schools and classes
Nursery schools and classes 64, 100, 104, 105, 112, 114
Nutrition 9, 43, 61, 63, 66

Offending see juvenile crime
Opting out (hospitals) 7-8
Opting out (schools) 9
Orkney Inquiry 12, 78-80, 83
Outcomes (of intervention) 89, 92-6, 112, 120, 125, 128, 130, 131
Outreach 122, 123

Pakistani families 41
Panmure House 143
Parent education 10, 92-3
Parental leave 18, 21, 27, 32
Parental involvement
 - in early years centres 93, 112
 - in schools 9, 10, 129, 142
Parenting skills 91
Parenting stress (PSI) 109, 110
Parenting styles 46, 90-1, 94
Parents' views of social work services 127-8, 129-30

Parents' Charter 9
Parents' responsibilities 3, 20, 28, 48, 60, 73, 80, 81, 82, 100, 136, 150, 154
Parents' rights 3, 10, 21, 81, 83, 154
Partnerships
 - between agencies (see also Inter-agency work) 10, 88
 - with parents 10, 30, 76, 78, 93, 133, 142, 154
Participation 10, 30, 64, 66, 67, 71, 73, 84, 106, 121, 143, 154, 155, 157
Part-time employment 2, 60, 65
Perry Pre-school Programme 93
Personal social services see Social services; Social work
Playgroups 90, 100
Pluralism (of welfare services) 7, 30, 152-4
Police 78, 79, 140
'Policing' the family 12, 72-3, 76-9, 82, 83, 150
Population policy 18-9
Portugal 19, 25, 27, 29
Post-modernism 151-3
Poverty xv, 26, 32, 48, 53-70
 Causes of poverty 5, 42, 48, 56, 60, 69, 90
 Impact on families 5, 18, 48, 53, 56, 61-4, 65, 90, 92, 107, 108, 114, 156
 Meaning of poverty 42, 53, 55-6
 Numbers of families in poverty xiv, 42, 53-4, 107-9, 156
 Relief of poverty 19, 27, 65-6, 77, 156
 Risks of poverty 27, 42, 48, 54, 59-61, 156
Preschool services, provision see Early years provision
Prevention, preventive services 11, 23, 30, 31, 72, 77, 87-8, 94, 101, 120, 121
Privacy 3, 22, 40, 42, 48, 71, 82, 100, 101
Private law 73, 80-1, 82, 154
Privatisation 4
Projects for families see Family projects
Professionals (and support) 84, 110-1, 132
Promotion of children's welfare 81, 87, 90, 96
Provision of services 59, 71, 84, 113, 132
Psychosocial development 121, 125, 131

Public law 73, 81, 83, 154
Public transport 6, 7
Purchaser-provider split 7, 144, 153
Psychologists 122, 124, 139, 140, 143
Psychiatrists 92, 122, 124

Reconstituted families 42, 47
Relatives (see also Kin)
 - and child care 110, 111, 113, 114
Reporters 11, 74, 75, 76, 80, 91
Representation (of children) 75-6, 81-4
Research 88, 90, 91, 93, 94, 104-5, 120-1, 137-8, 141, 157
Residential care 21, 30-1, 74, 120, 129-31
Residential care staff 122, 129
Residential schools 31, 122-3, 124, 129, 130, 131, 138
Residential units see Residential care
Respite care 8, 21, 81, 130
Revenu Minimum D'Insertion (R.M.I.) 19
Rosemount Project 65-8
Royston 65
Rural areas (families living in) 7, 9, 56
Rutter scale 121, 125, 131

Safeguarders 75-6, 81, 82, 83
Save the Children Fund 64, 65
Scandinavia 18, 20, 21, 24, 27, 28, 29, 41, 51, 155
Schools see also Residential schools; Education: Special Education
 School Boards 9
 School exclusion 10
 School-home relationships 10, 47, 79, 142-3
 School league tables 10
 School liaison groups 139, 143-4
 School meals 59, 65
 School non-attendance 74, 137, 138, 150
 School placing requests 9, 62
 School related problems 9, 10, 91, 92, 121, 137
 School self-government 9, 155
 Schools and child abuse 79
Scotland xiv, xv, 1, 3, 9, 11, 12, 13, 32, 53, 56, 61, 72-84, 99, 119, 149
Scotland's Children (White Paper) 81-3, 101, 135, 137, 155
Scottish Child Care Law Review 136
Scottish Law Commission 80-3
Scottish legal system 11, 12
Scottish Low Pay Unit 57
Scottish Office 83, 135
Screening of children 89, 94-5
Section 12, Social Work (Scotland) Act, 1968 72, 81, 83, 84
Self care 120
Self confidence, self esteem 61, 66, 68, 94, 124, 125
Self-employed people 57, 60
Self presentation 120
Separation (marital) 41, 42, 73, 155
Service-finance packages 23
Sexual abuse see Child sexual abuse
Sexual relationships 41, 47-8
Single parents see Lone parents
Sheriffs 74, 75, 79, 80, 81
Sick children 61
Significant harm 88, 96
Social class 9, 44, 62, 90
Social control (of families) 12, 77, 96, 150-3
Social Fund 53, 59, 63
Social integration 3, 68, 114
Social isolation 67, 111-3
Social networks 99, 102, 110-1, 113, 133, 152
Social policies 1, 22, 24-5, 31
Social policing xv, 12, 76-9, 83, 96, 150
Social relationships 101-2, 113, 115, 121
Social services departments 12, 103, 121, 124
Social services and education 12, 30, 124, 132, 136, 140
Social Services Inspectorate 88
Social security xiv, 19, 23, 25, 26, 28, 32, 55-6, 98
Social support 30, 94, 101-2, 104, 153
Social work 12, 91-2, 120-4
Social work assessment 89, 91
Social work departments 78, 21, 124, 144, 154
Social work roles 12, 13, 75, 78, 79, 83, 91-2, 120, 121, 124, 131, 132
Social workers 75, 78, 79, 80, 83, 84, 124, 125, 126, 127, 130, 140-1, 144
Social Work (Scotland) Act, 1968 11, 72, 73, 74, 78, 80, 81
Social work training 83, 131-2
Spain 20, 23, 25, 26, 27, 31, 41
Special education 122, 124, 139, 143
Standards of living 59, 156

State intervention in family life 2, 3, 4, 11, 12, 17-34, 48, 64, 100-1, 151-2
Step-families see Reconstituted families
Strathclyde Region 65, 139
Stress (in families) 1, 13, 56, 64, 102, 103, 109-10, 113
Supervision (at home) 72, 74, 123, 125, 126-7, 132
Sweden 17, 20, 21, 22, 24, 25, 27, 28, 29, 30, 31, 48
Switzerland 17, 24, 25, 29, 41

Targeting 8, 17, 19, 20, 26-8, 88, 114, 115
Taxation see also Fiscal policy 20, 21, 26, 59
Tax relief 18, 19, 26, 29
Tayside Region 140-4
Teachers 79, 137, 141, 150
Technological change 156-7
Teenagers see Young people; Adolescence
Thatcherism 4, 152
Therapeutic services 11, 64, 124
Training (for employment) 64-5, 66-7
Transport 6, 7
TRYST groups 140-4

UN Convention on the Rights of the Child xiv, 2, 31, 68, 71, 76, 80, 81, 82, 83, 84, 135, 155, 156
Unemployment 5, 43, 56-8, 60, 62, 65, 108, 114, 140
Universal provision (of services) 20, 90, 92, 96, 115, 150
USA 1, 23, 27, 30, 93, 95, 141, 151

Violence 90, 91
Vocational training 65-6

Voluntary organisations 30, 139, 143, 152, 153
Volunteers 93, 94, 123

Wages 25, 57
Wales see England & Wales
Welfare approach to juvenile crime 11, 12, 30, 74
Welfare benefits 13, 18, 19, 20, 21, 24-6, 41, 55-7, 59, 61, 65-7, 92, 150
Welfare of the child 2, 3, 4, 5, 8, 12, 18, 74, 87-8, 135
Welfare pluralism 7, 30, 152-4
Welfare states 1, 2, 22, 24, 33, 152-3, 157
Well-being 109-10
Western Europe xiv, 17-30, 149, 150
Women's roles as carers 2, 8, 13, 20
Women's roles as homemakers 2, 7, 22, 27
Women's paid employment 2, 20, 21, 25, 27, 28, 29, 32, 43, 45, 61, 65, 107
Work 2, 5, 18, 20, 21, 22, 27, 31, 65
Working parents 32, 99, 108, 114-5, 156
Working Together Under the Children Act 1989 88

Youth 12, 31, 119, 135-45
Young people xv, 11, 119-134, 135-45
    Young people and poverty 53, 56
    Young people's relationships with social workers 119-20, 122, 127-8
    Young people's views of residential and foster care 128-31
    Young people's views of supervision 126-8
Youth strategies xvi, 138-40, 144-5

HMSO

HMSO publications are available from:

HMSO Publications Centre
(Mail, fax and telephone orders only)
PO Box 276, London, SW8 5DT
Telephone orders 0171-873 9090
General enquiries 0171-873 0011
(queuing system in operation for both numbers)
Fax orders 0171-873 8200

HMSO Bookshops
71 Lothian Road, Edinburgh, EH3 9AZ
0131-228 4181 Fax 0131-229 2734
49 High Holborn, London, WC1V 6HB
0171-873 0011 Fax 0171-873 1326 (counter service only)
68-69 Bull Street, Birmingham, B4 6AD
0121-236 9696 Fax 0121-236 9699
33 Wine Street, Bristol, BS1 2BQ
0117 9264306 Fax 0117 9294515
9-21 Princess Street, Manchester, M60 8AS
0161-834 7201 Fax 0161-833 0634
16 Arthur Street, Belfast, BT1 4GD
01232 238451 Fax 01232 235401
The HMSO Oriel Bookshop,
The Friary, CArdiff CF1 4AA
01222 395548 Fax 01222 384347

HMSO's Accredited Agents
(see Yellow Pages)

and through good booksellers

Printed in Great Britain for HMSO Scotland by
CC No 20249 IOC 6/95